The Implementer's Starter Kit, Second Edition

THE IMPLEMENTER'S STARTER KIT, SECOND EDITION

How to Plan and Execute Organizational Change Like a Master, Even If You Aren't One Yet

Wendy Hirsch

Wendy Hirsch Consulting, LLC
Saint Petersburg, FL

© 2019 Wendy Hirsch Consulting, LLC. All rights reserved.

ISBN 978-1-7332472-0-7 (Paperback, 2nd Edition)
ISBN 978-1-7332472-1-4 (Ebook, 2nd Edition)

Cover Design: Alicia Tatone
Interior Graphics: Kirsten McKinney
Proofreading: Joanna Pyke

Wendy Hirsch Consulting, LLC
4604 49th Street, #1010
Saint Petersburg, FL 33709
wendyhirsch.com

Disclaimer

Although the information and recommendations in this book are presented in good faith and believed to be correct, Wendy Hirsch Consulting LLC makes no representations or warranties as to the completeness or accuracy of the information. All content provided in this book is for informational purposes only. Information is supplied "as is" and on the condition that the persons receiving same will make their own determination of its suitability for their purposes prior to use.

The publisher and author of this book will not be liable for any errors or omissions in this information, nor for any losses, injuries, or damages from the use of this information. These terms and conditions are subject to change at any time with or without notice.

CONTENTS

Introduction
Does This Seem Familiar? ... 9
This Book Is for You ... 10
What You'll Learn ... 12
How This Book Is Organized ... 15

Part I: WHY
The Need for a Comprehensive Approach ... 19
Why "just do it" doesn't work

Case Study: Principles in Action ... 25
Lessons from a school-based implementation in California

Part II: WHAT
What Is Implementation? ... 33
The three I's of implementation

Using a Framework to Guide You ... 37
See the forest for the trees

A Brief Tour of the Framework ... 40
Components, Roles, Phases, Context

Part III: WHEN
Five Phases of Implementation ... 49
Decide, Prepare, Execute, Improve, Maintain

Phases: A Versatile and Valuable Tool ... 53
Clarify location, direction, and duration

Part IV: HOW
Desired Outcomes ... 67
The vision and rationale for the change

The Innovation ... 76
What you implement

Performance Monitoring and Measurement ... 87
How to understand what's working, what's not, and why

Training and Coaching ... 103
Build skills and confidence

Infrastructure	115
Physical, administrative, and project management supports	
Communication	129
The exchange of information and ideas	

Part V: WHO

The Implementation Team	141
Mandate, skills, and structure	
Leadership	160
The sponsor, governance body, and middle management	
End Users	179
Change can't happen without them	
Stakeholders	188
Influencers, customers, and more	

Part VI: WHERE

Context	205
Where you implement matters	

A Final Note...

Make the most of it	221
Implementation Checklist	225
Implementation Framework	229
List of Figures	230
Bibliography	232
Acknowledgements	247
About the Author	248

INTRODUCTION

DOES THIS SEEM FAMILIAR?

Have you ever finished celebrating the approval of a new strategy or major initiative and thought, "Now, what?!"

Or had a great idea to improve your organization, followed by a sinking feeling when you asked yourself, "But how would we *do* that?"

Or finished rolling out a new tool or practice only to find no one using it after a few months?

You are not alone.

When implementation is an afterthought or approached with a quick and dirty ethos, things may get done, but they rarely produce results. If you don't get the intended benefits from your effort, can you genuinely call it a success?

There are no silver bullet solutions guaranteed to make all change implementations successful. However, there are sound practices and principles that, when used consistently, can increase your chances of truly making a difference in your organization.

That's what this book is about.

THIS BOOK IS FOR YOU

This book is for those new to change implementation as well as those looking for new perspectives to bring to their change efforts. Because whether you are in the early days of your career or have a wealth of professional experience, implementation can be a challenge if you don't have a defined approach.

Although the majority of this book is directed at the person leading the implementation team, sometimes called an implementation lead, project manager, or change lead, the ideas and tips offered are relevant to anyone who is keen on better understanding the art and science of implementation. We'll cover the fundamentals of effective implementation management, such as designing the implementation approach, planning for execution, monitoring progress, interacting with leadership and stakeholders, and developing your team.

Specifically, this book is for you, if...

- You have technical or managerial experience, but are new to implementation and are **unsure where to start.**
- You are an experienced implementer looking for a fresh outlook or alternative approaches to **improve your results.**
- You are beginning your career or are looking to advance and want to **build a new skill set.**
- You are an experienced implementer but want a deeper understanding of the fundamentals of implementation

so that you **can coach others.**
- You are an executive or manager supervising implementation staff and want a **stronger foundation in the core concepts** of implementation.

WHAT YOU'LL LEARN

My goal is to provide you with a firm grounding in the fundamentals of effective implementation. The ideas presented in this book are based on my 20 years of practical experience, as well as a robust body of academic research about what works in implementation. Importantly, the principles and methods outlined are adaptable and can be used to support the implementation of all kinds of organizational change, such as new processes, practices, strategies, or tools.

The book is designed to help you build confidence in three areas:

1. What you need to do: I introduce a simple framework that provides a blueprint you can use to plan and execute your next implementation.

2. Why you should do it: I explain the purpose of each part of the framework and how it supports effective implementation.

3. How to get started: In addition to theory, I provide examples, tools, and other "how to" information throughout the book. At the end of most chapters, I offer a list of Starter Steps to help you begin applying the ideas presented.

What you won't find in this book and why

Equally important to what you will find in this book, is what you will not, such as:

A cookie-cutter approach. Context is a significant factor in implementation. The ability to tailor your methods to your operating environment is an essential skill for any implementer. For that reason, I focus as much on best principles, as best practices.[1] A strong grounding in such principles will equip you to adapt to the variety of contexts and types of implementation you will face on the job.

Deep-dives into technical topics. A proficient implementer is one that has developed expertise in a variety of domains, such as project management, team leadership, measurement, and communications. However, a full exploration of such technical domains is beyond the scope of this book. Rather, I take a "first things first" approach. I aim to clarify the fundamental skills you need and provide examples, tools, and practical action steps to help you begin applying them in your work. In my view, that's plenty to get you started.

Requirements for specific types of implementation. I aim to help you build a base of knowledge that you can apply to all sorts of change implementation. As such, this book does not address requirements for particular types of implementation, such as Enterprise Resource Planning (ERP) systems or evidence-based health and education programs.

Notes

1. I was introduced to the term "best principles" in the work of Mary Northridge and Sara Metcalf. They note: "Best principles, as distinct from the more customary term 'best practices', are used to underscore the need to extract the core issues from the context in which they are embedded in order to better ensure that they are transferable across settings." See Northridge, M. E., & Metcalf, S. S. (2016). Enhancing implementation science by applying best principles of systems science. *Health Research Policy and Systems, 14*(1), 74. doi: 10.1186/s12961-016-0146-8

HOW THIS BOOK IS ORGANIZED

This book is designed to be a partner to you throughout your next implementation. Although you can read it straight through, it may be most valuable to use it as a reference book. You can delve into topics based on where you are in your current implementation or the skills you want to strengthen.

To help you do that, I organized the book into six parts that relate to the core questions you will face when designing and executing any change implementation — Why? What? When? How? Who? Where?

The first three parts — Why, What, and When — provide an overview of the foundational aspects of implementation to ensure you have a firm grounding on which to build your approach.

Part I — Why: You'll learn why it's important to take a disciplined and informed approach to implementation, rather than making it up as you go along.

Part II — What: You'll get acquainted with the basics of the implementation framework that forms the foundation of this book.

Part III — When: You'll learn the five phases of implementation, as well as how to focus your actions based on each phase.

The last three sections — How, Who, and Where — cover the individual elements of the framework, each of which will be relevant to you at various times during the planning and execution of your effort.

Part IV — How: You'll learn about the tools you use to implement. Specifically, each chapter in this section focuses on a different component of the implementation framework, such as infrastructure, measurement, or training.

Part V — Who: You'll learn about the critical roles people play in the implementation process, what's required of those who fill these roles, and how to engage with them to successfully execute your implementation.

Part VI — Where: You'll learn how to identify critical contextual factors, both internal and external, to inform your implementation approach.

To help you better understand the concepts presented in each section, you'll find brief case studies and example tools throughout the book. Additionally, most chapters conclude with a set of Starter Steps designed to help you begin putting the methods presented to work for you.

Finally, updates made to the second edition include:

- An expanded chapter on Leadership, which now includes a discussion of the role of middle managers in leading change.
- A new chapter on Communication; a topic that was previously integrated throughout the book.
- A revision of the Context chapter, including an updated approach to context analysis.

PART I: WHY

In this section, we explore the answer to our first question: Why do we need to take a comprehensive approach to implementation? We also discuss the fundamental principles of effective implementation using a case study of a state-wide education implementation.

THE NEED FOR A COMPREHENSIVE APPROACH

Why "just do it" doesn't work

When implementing any change, you first need to clarify why you are doing it. You need to be explicit about the purpose of the change and what you want to achieve.

You should be able to answer the same questions about your implementation approach. What is the purpose of adopting a comprehensive rather than an ad-hoc strategy when implementing? What do you achieve by being proactive and purposeful in your efforts?

Knowing the answers to these questions is vital for a few reasons.

First, when leading an implementation, you need to be confident in your plan of attack. That doesn't mean you won't be unsure at some points or won't make mistakes. You will. Rather, what I'm talking about is the underlying conviction that when it comes down to it, you know what you need to do and why you need to do it.

Second, you will, at some point, work with leaders who believe that when something is implemented you "just do it" — that elbow grease and chutzpah are all that's needed. In such situations, a keen understanding of effective implementation methods can help you to convince those with power that unless you direct that chutzpah in a thoughtful way, it's unlikely to create much value.

Third, when you demonstrate expertise in implementation, it may have a beneficial impact on end users. Research indicates there is an association between staff perceptions of management competence to implement change and stress, uncertainty, and skepticism during a period of change.[1]

Finally, the last reason is that the answers to these questions exist! What makes for effective implementation is *not* a huge mystery. True, there is no fool-proof solution to all implementation challenges, and probably never will be. But there are strong indications that some things work better than others.

Implementation failures led to the development of a wide body of research

As far back as the 1940s, academics were theorizing about organizational change.[2] In the 1970s, researchers began looking at specific tactics people use to implement change in organizations, often focusing on the role of management.[3]

In the 1990s, researchers in healthcare sought to understand why medical innovations were not being used. They were frustrated that practices, which had been tested and found effective in studies, were not benefiting patients. The reason? Often it was because medical personnel in hospitals and doctors' offices weren't adequately implementing them. This research became a field of study known as implementation science or implementation research.[4]

Over the last 20 years or so, investigations into what makes for effective implementation have expanded beyond healthcare interventions, to look at education and social services. The wave of high-stakes implementation related to Enterprise Resource Planning (ERP) systems has also produced its own body of research.

Taken in combination, these investigations into what works in implementation (and what doesn't) have yielded some themes, but no guaranteed prescriptions, for effective implementation. One resoundingly clear idea in the research, however, is that it's just as important to focus on *how* you implement, as it is on *what* you implement.

Effective implementation requires skillful use of a system of complementary parts

Mastering the "how" of implementation requires the development of a system and the ability to use that system effectively. To better understand this idea, let's look at the example of the carmaker Toyota. In recent years, safety recalls put a dent in Toyota's rock-solid reputation for quality. However, in the 1980s, the car company became famous not only for the cars it produced but also for how it made them.

In fact, at that time Toyota surprised everyone by regularly giving tours to engineers from competing carmakers. In particular, these tours provided a close-up look at Toyota's famed continuous improvement process. But, Toyota didn't feel there was any risk in showing their competition precisely *what* they did. Why?

As John Shook, an American who worked for Toyota in Japan, put it: "Remember how Vince Lombardi always said he would share his playbook with anyone, but nobody could execute like the old Green Bay Packers? It is the same thing with Toyota. Everybody has techniques and practices, but nobody has a system like Toyota's."[5]

Toyota understood what implementation research shows us — *how* you implement matters as much as *what* you implement.

Further, in creating the "Toyota Way," the company demonstrated the benefits of integrating skills and practices into a well-functioning, systematic approach.

Effective implementation requires an approach grounded in best principles

As the example of Toyota demonstrates, a systematic approach to implementation is required. However, this need not be complicated. An effective implementation often has a simplicity to it, which is rooted in the principles that support it.

The method outlined in the remainder of this book is grounded in several core principles, including:

- Start by defining the problem you are trying to solve and how you'll know when you've solved it.
- Identify the best solution to the problem, investigating not only the evidence supporting various options but also your capacity to implement them.
- Define the solution with enough specificity that everyone can understand what it is and what it isn't.
- Develop a plan and assemble a diverse team to execute it.
- Support adoption by end users with training and ongoing coaching.
- Work closely with — and listen to — stakeholders at all levels.
- Pay attention to context.

These principles may strike you as common sense. However, for many people working in implementation, the problem is not recognizing that these things are important in the abstract. It's being disciplined and organized enough to do them. In practice, our enthusiasm for a new solution or our ambition to achieve big things can entice us to cast aside common sense for quick-fix approaches, which rarely produce promised results.

Before we delve further into the details of the implementation framework that forms the core of this book, we'll first review a case study through the lens of these principles. This example demonstrates what can happen when you implement with good intentions, but without a comprehensive approach.

Notes

1. See Oreg, S., Vakola, M., & Armenakis, A. (2011). Change recipients' reactions to organizational change: A 60-year review of quantitative studies. *The Journal of Applied Behavioral Science, 47*(4). doi: 10.1177/0021886310396550
2. For an overview of Kurt Lewin's change theory and a summary of six decades of additional work on change, see Burnes, B. (2004). Kurt Lewin and the planned approach to change: A re-appraisal. *Journal of Management Studies, 41*(6), 977-1002. doi: 10.1111/j.1467-6486.2004.00463.x
3. For a helpful summary of implementation research in the 1970s, see Nutt, P. C. (1986). Tactics of implementation. *Academy of Management Journal, 29*(2), 230-261. doi: 10.2307/256187
4. For an overview of implementation science see Bauer, M. S., Damschroder, L., Hagedorn, H., Smith, J., & Kilbourne, A. M. (2015). An introduction to implementation science for the non-specialist. *BMC Psychology, 3*(1), 32. doi: 10.1186/s40359-015-0089-9
5. Quoted from Taylor, A., & Kahn, J. (1997). How Toyota defies gravity. *Fortune, 136* (11), 100-106. Retrieved from http://archive.fortune.com/magazines/fortune/fortune_archive/1997/12/08/234926/index.htm

CASE STUDY: PRINCIPLES IN ACTION

Lessons from a school-based implementation in California

In the mid-1990s, the Governor of California secured passage of legislation that aimed to increase student performance in math and reading by reducing the size of classes in elementary grades throughout the state.[1] This initiative in California was inspired, at least in part, by a pilot program in Tennessee called Project STAR. Project STAR had garnered national attention for impacting student outcomes through the adoption of smaller class sizes.

The class-size reduction program in California was voluntary and offered to all elementary schools throughout the state. The program provided schools with $650 for each student in a class with fewer than 20 other kids. The dollar amount offered was the same for all schools, regardless of the size of their classes at the start of the program.

By the end of the first year, nearly 90% of first-grade students in California public schools were in classes of reduced size, with almost 60% of second graders in such classes. The program also proved to be wildly popular with teachers and parents alike. So, it seems, the California program got things done. Class sizes were smaller; teachers and parents were happy.

However, the purpose of the program was to improve student outcomes. You may wonder, how did the program do in those terms? Unfortunately, after two years, and spending $2.5B, the California effort demonstrated negligible impact on student outcomes.

Why was a program that was successful in improving student outcomes in Tennessee, less so in California? There are probably many reasons, but when we get into the details, it seems at least part of the cause had to do with a failure to adhere to the best principles of effective implementation. Let's look at a few examples.

PRINCIPLE: Evaluate potential solutions based on technical appropriateness and your capacity to implement

The California effort focused mainly on copying *what* was done in the Tennessee program, i.e., the innovation of small class sizes. It does not appear, however, that the California legislators studied *how* this innovation was implemented in Tennessee before offering it to all schools in the state. Nor did they question whether the innovation of small classroom sizes was the most cost-effective means to increase literacy scores in the context of California schools. Perhaps reducing class sizes was *a* solution to lagging student outcomes, rather than *the* solution to that problem.

California was not alone in embracing class-size reduction as a solution to its achievement challenges. Many states chose to implement this innovation, although reportedly not many studied its efficacy before implementing it.

PRINCIPLE: Engage with stakeholders at all levels and plan before acting

The California legislation to reduce class sizes passed in July 1996, less than two months before the start of the school year. Consider the practical challenges this posed for school administrators. If you want smaller class sizes, but have the same number of students, you have to increase the number of available teachers and classrooms. In fact, implementing the program required securing some 18,000 additional classrooms and 12,000 new teachers in just a few months. This proved to be an impossible task.

Eventually, due to the teacher shortage prompted by smaller class sizes, the Governor signed legislation that relaxed teacher certification standards, raising questions about instruction quality.

PRINCIPLE: Define what you are implementing and implement it consistently

Although the Tennessee and California programs were both class-size reduction efforts, what was implemented in each state was quite different.

In California, districts were given the discretion to implement the program to varying degrees. For example, one school could reduce the size of all K-3 classes, while another could choose to do so only in first and second grades. Notably, at its start, the California program involved *150 times* the number of students that were part of the Tennessee effort. Therefore, although class sizes were reduced, what was considered a small class in California was still much larger than it had been in the Tennessee program. Further, due to a lack of available, qualified staff and suitable space, some classes in California were led by uncertified teachers and in places not intended to be used as classrooms, such as gyms and libraries.

Should one assume that two programs that were similar in name, but not in practice, would produce similarly promising results? Likely not.

PRINCIPLE: Support adoption through training and ongoing coaching to end users

States that evaluated the effectiveness of their class-size reduction programs found that significant outcomes could result from this intervention. However, these outcomes were dependent on several factors *beyond classroom size*, including a supply of qualified teachers, suitable classroom space, rigorous curricula, and professional development for teachers.

Helping teachers put good practices in place is essential to getting those practices to have an impact on kids.

What happened in California is not unique

Even if you don't have professional experience in government or education, if you've worked in an organization, you can probably name a few implementations that fell short for some of the reasons highlighted in this case.

The basics of good implementation are commonly overlooked, even in a highly public, big-ticket effort such as this one in California. Unfortunately, as this case also demonstrates, quick-fix approaches to implementation are a risky proposition if you are looking to achieve results beyond popularity.

Imagine how different things may have been if a few trained implementers had been involved in this effort from the beginning. In the next section, we'll delve further into what that might look like.

Notes

1. This case was adapted from information provided in Bohrnstedt, G. W., & Stecher, B. M. (2002). What we have learned about class size reduction in California. Sacramento: California Department of Education. Retrieved from http://www.classize.org/techreport/CSRYear4_final.pdf, and Stecher, B. M. & Bohrnstedt, G. W. (Eds.). (2002). Class size reduction in California: Findings from 1999–00 and 2000–01. Sacramento, CA: California Department of Education. Retrieved from https://www.classsizematters.org/wp-content/uploads/2012/11/year3_technicalreport.pdf

PART II: WHAT

In this section, we delve into our second question: What is implementation? We review the implementation framework that forms the foundation of this book to give you a bird's-eye view of the pieces and parts that make up an effective implementation system.

WHAT IS IMPLEMENTATION?

The three I's of implementation

I define implementation in a multidimensional way through what I call the three "I's" of implementation — Implementation, Innovation, and Integrity.[1] Let's review each in turn.

Implementation: A dual-purpose process

Implementation (v): To make something active and effective.

As used in this book, implementation refers to a process through which you put something in place within an organization (make it active) and ensure it produces results (make it effective). You must do both.

Although there are many definitions of the word implementation, I like this one because it reflects its dual aims. When leading an implementation, it's essential to keep the results you want to achieve top of mind. Failing to do so can cause you and your stakeholders to mistake activity for outcomes.

Take the example of the California class-size reduction effort mentioned in the previous section. Although class sizes for grades K-3 were reduced in the majority of schools in the state, the desired impact on student achievement was limited. They made something active — smaller class sizes — but it was not effective because the new practice did not produce the intended results.

Innovation: What you implement

Innovation (n): The change being implemented.

The innovation is the new thing you put in place when you implement. It could be a strategy, practice, process, technology, policy, or something else! In the case study outlined in the previous section, the innovation being implemented was smaller class sizes in grades K-3.

Some people refer to the innovation as an intervention or simply a change. I prefer the term innovation for a few reasons.

First, the word innovation signals the inherent novelty in implementation. When we implement, we are almost always introducing something new, which means we are entering uncharted territory. We are encouraging people to alter what they do, how they think, and how they behave. Many people find this challenging. They are not accustomed to the innovation, and as a result, they may be a bit clumsy with it at first. There is a learning curve inherent in any implementation; patience is essential.

Second, I like the positive implication of the word innovation. It's exciting, fresh, and full of optimism. Implementation can be hard, but it is also full of possibility! That's important to remember, particularly when things get difficult, which they will.

Integrity: How you implement for results

Integrity (n): Faithfulness or adherence to the defined innovation.

Integrity refers to how much the innovation is modified during the implementation process. People will customize, adjust, and make the innovation their own. On the one hand, this is productive because it helps end users to develop a sense of ownership and control. The risk with such customizations is that they can result in many different innovations being implemented, which can have significant implications for the outcomes you achieve.

The integrity of your implementation will be impacted by how well you define the innovation, train people how to use it, coach them through rough spots, and monitor your efforts to identify necessary adjustments.

To better understand this concept, let's look again at the case study on class-size reduction, where the innovation was arguably not implemented with integrity. We saw that classes were made smaller in the California program, but, on average, remained much larger than they were in the Tennessee program on which the California effort was modeled. Additionally, in California, each district was given leeway to implement the class-size reduction in just a few grades or all K-3 classes. Further, the reduction in class sizes caused a sharp increase in demand for space and teachers. As a result, many classes were taught by uncertified teachers and in areas not intended to be used as classrooms.

These are all examples of variations that reduced the integrity of the implementation in California and likely impacted the results achieved. We'll discuss this topic in depth in the Innovation chapter.

Notes

1. Terms are not standard in the fields of implementation and change management; others may define implementation differently.

USING A FRAMEWORK TO GUIDE YOU

See the forest for the trees

As we saw in the example of the California class-size reduction program, implementation undertaken without a thoughtful, integrated approach can put the achievement of desired results at risk. However, it may seem that there's so much to do that you could never keep it all straight. Don't throw your hands up just yet! That's where a framework can be helpful.

A framework acts like a blueprint or structure that organizes the core parts of a comprehensive implementation approach. It provides a big picture reference that can help you to stay on track.

This is not the only framework

I developed a simple framework to help professionals like you make sense of the inherent complexity of implementation, without being overwhelmed by it. This framework is based on areas of consistency that I identified in research, as well as my experience leading implementations over the last 20 years. However, please know this is just one framework among many that describe the implementation process.[1]

You need it all, but it all doesn't have to be perfect

Although the framework is made up of various pieces and parts, it functions as a whole. All of the elements are necessary for successful implementation — you can't just focus on those that are easy or that align with your preferences. (I know because I've tried; it doesn't work!)

That's because the parts are complementary. They are interdependent, so if you take out one piece, your system will be lopsided. However, the parts are also compensatory, which means you don't have to be equally stellar in all areas. You can be a bit weak in one and stronger in another. Things will balance out, as long as you've covered everything to some degree.[2] So, the other thing to remember is that you don't need to be perfect in all areas. (That's impossible anyway!)

Notes

1. For an overview of various frameworks, see Meyers, D. C., Durlak, J.A., & Wandersman, A. (2012). The quality implementation framework: A synthesis of critical steps in the implementation process. *American Journal of Community Psychology, 50*(3-4), 462-480. doi: 10.1007/s10464-012-9522-x. For a summary of research particular to strategy implementation, see Noble, C. H. (1999). The eclectic roots of strategy implementation research. *Journal of Business Research, 45*(2), 119-134. doi: 10.1016/S0148-2963(97)00231-2
2. For more on the complementary and compensatory nature of implementation components or factors, see Bertram, R. M., Blase, K. A., & Fixsen, D. L. (2015). Improving programs and outcomes: Implementation frameworks and organization change. *Research on Social Work Practice, 25*, 477- 487. doi:10.1177/1049731514537687

A BRIEF TOUR OF THE FRAMEWORK

Components, Roles, Phases, Context

Let's take a tour of the implementation framework to familiarize you with its essential elements. In later parts of the book, we'll dive deeper into each area of the framework and review how to apply it to your implementation efforts.

The framework is composed of four parts:

- **Components,** which are the tools, both physical and conceptual, that you use to implement. Components provide structure to your implementation.
- **Roles,** which refer to the people involved in driving the implementation forward.
- **Phases,** which are the various stages of the implementation life cycle.
- **Context,** which refers to internal and external factors that can impact the implementation.

We'll discuss each briefly throughout this chapter. For a summary of the framework, see Figure 1. (For a printable summary, visit the resources section of my website at wendyhirsch.com.)

THE IMPLEMENTATION FRAMEWORK
Four Elements of a Comprehensive Approach

COMPONENTS — WHY, WHAT & HOW
The tools you use to implement. Components provide definition and structure to the implementation.

- **Desired Outcomes** — The vision and rationale for the change
- **The Innovation** — What you are implementing
- **Measurement & Monitoring** — How you know if you've achieved your desired outcomes
- **Training & Coaching** — How you teach and reinforce new skills
- **Plan & Infrastructure** — How things will get done

Communication — How you share information and ideas

ROLES — WHO
The people who create and use components to drive the implementation forward.

- **Implementation Team** — Plans, executes, and troubleshoots
- **End Users** — Actively use the innovation
- **Leadership** — Inspires, explains, and reinforces
- **Stakeholders** — Influence, support, or challenge the effort

PHASES — WHEN
Key stages in the life cycle of the implementation. Phases help you focus your efforts appropriately. They are more iterative than linear.

Decide → Prepare → Execute → Improve → Maintain

CONTEXT — WHERE
Aspects of the internal and external environment that may impact the implementation.

wendyhirsch.com

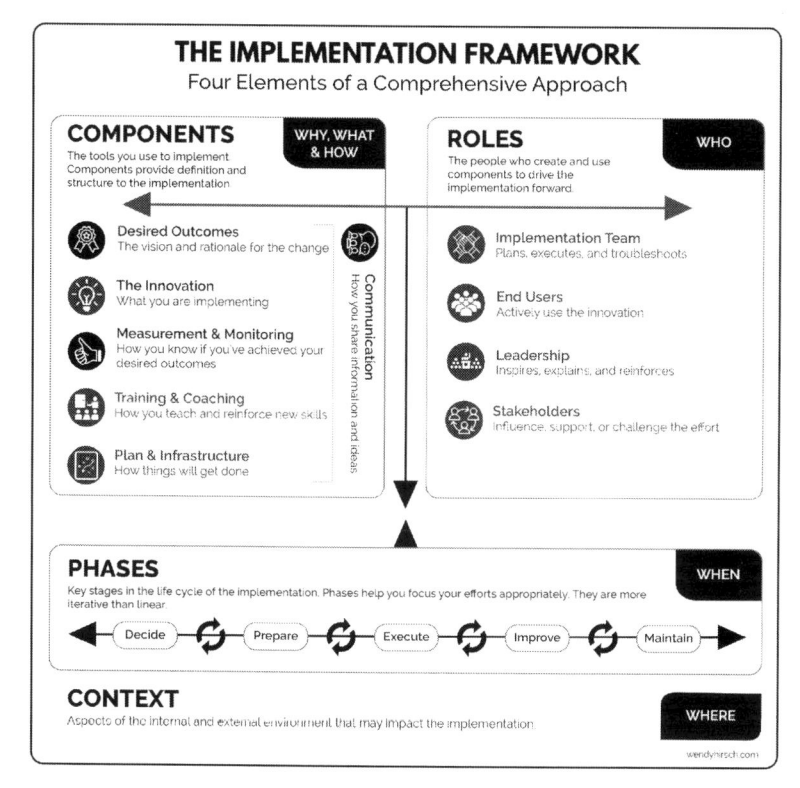

Figure 1 — Implementation Framework

Components — Why, What, and How

Components are the tools you use to implement. They provide structure and definition to your effort. In my framework, components refer to six things: desired outcomes, the innovation, measurement and monitoring, training and coaching, infrastructure, and communication.

Desired outcomes help to clarify why you are implementing the change in the first place. They are a minimum set of priority results the organization expects to attain as a consequence of the implementation.

The **innovation** is what you are implementing. It should be selected based on its fit to your need as well as the capacity of your organization to implement it. The innovation should also be defined with sufficient specificity to clarify both what you *are* and *are not* implementing.

COMPONENTS

The tools you use to implement. Components provide definition and structure to the implementation.

WHY, WHAT & HOW

- **Desired Outcomes** — What you want to achieve and why
- **The Innovation** — What you are implementing
- **Measurement & Monitoring** — How you know if you've achieved your desired outcomes
- **Training & Coaching** — How you teach and reinforce new skills
- **Plan & Infrastructure** — How things will get done

Communication — How you share information and ideas

wendyhirsch.com

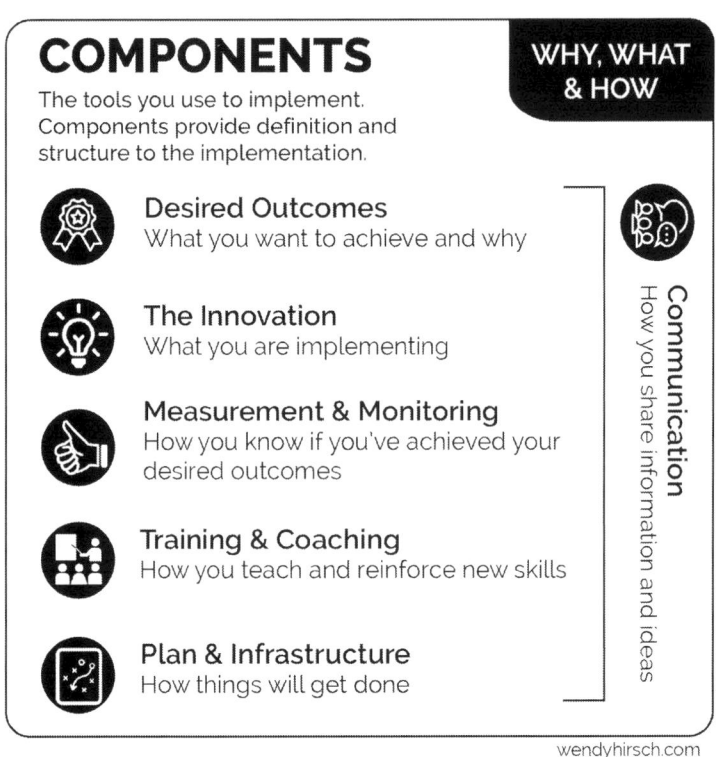

Figure 2 – Components

Performance **measurement and monitoring** involve setting goals and collecting, reviewing, and responding to feedback about your effort. This allows you to identify what's going well, what's not, and what you need to do to improve. Ultimately, measurement and monitoring enable you to evaluate if the implementation has been successful.

In all efforts, **training and coaching** provide essential knowledge and ongoing guidance to end users. Such support helps end users to adopt the innovation with integrity to produce desired results.

Every implementation requires a supportive **infrastructure** to give it form and clarify how things will be done. This includes physical enablers (e.g., a place for your team to work), administrative enablers (e.g., managers who provide time for staff to take part in implementation activities), and project management enablers (e.g., an implementation plan.)

Communication involves both formal and informal efforts to exchange information between all stakeholders involved in the change. It is both "push" and "pull" and includes not only words but also actions and behaviors. Communication is a distinct component of change implementation; however, it is also integral to the effective delivery of all other components.

Roles — Who

Make no mistake, although the components outlined previously are essential, implementation is fundamentally about people. Without people, nothing happens.

People play various roles to drive the implementation forward, including as part of the implementation team, end users, leadership, and stakeholders. Some of these roles require deep involvement in the effort, others only periodic participation. However, when leading an implementation, you must recognize, acknowledge, and engage with them all to some degree. Let's briefly review each role, as outlined in Figure 3.

Although there is an "I" in implementation, it is never a solo affair. You cannot do it alone! Creating an **implementation team** is critical. This team plans and executes most of the activities related to the implementation. It is primarily responsible for establishing and using the components discussed previously.

The implementation team also trains and supports **end users**, who are the people that will use the innovation or adopt the change you are implementing. The implementation team engages with **stakeholders**, such as those who will benefit from the implementation, as well as those who may want to influence it. Gathering input and feedback from these groups, and transforming it into decisions, plans, and actions are central activities of the implementation team and leadership.

ROLES — WHO

The people who create and use components to drive the implementation forward.

Implementation Team
Plans, executes, and troubleshoots

End Users
Actively use the innovation

Leadership
Inspires, explains, and reinforces

Stakeholders
Influence, support, or challenge the effort

wendyhirsch.com

Figure 3 — Roles

Organizational **leaders**, specifically those holding a sponsor or governance role, have a unique function in implementation. They are often best positioned to clarify the vision for the effort and to reinforce commitment during challenging times. Additionally, during change, middle managers are often called on to play an intermediary role between other leaders and staff.

Phases — When

Rather than a simple progression from start to finish, in reality, effective implementation is a multi-phased and iterative process. As such, the framework includes five phases that outline the stages you will move through, sometimes more than once, in any implementation journey. The five phases are: Decide, Prepare, Execute, Improve, and Maintain, as illustrated in Figure 4.

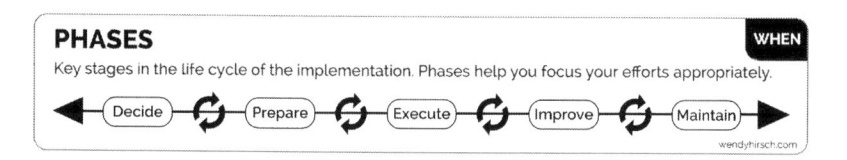

PHASES — **WHEN**
Key stages in the life cycle of the implementation. Phases help you focus your efforts appropriately.

Decide → Prepare → Execute → Improve → Maintain

Figure 4 — Phases

During the **Decide** phase, you establish the purpose of the effort, select the innovation that will be implemented, and agree on the resources that will be invested. Decisions made during this phase guide all subsequent planning.

The **Prepare** phase includes documenting the innovation, assembling the implementation team, creating a clear plan, and preparing for training and coaching.

All of this is done before the roll-out of the innovation during the **Execute** phase. Monitoring the implementation during execution is essential to provide data and feedback for the **Improve** phase, during which adjustments are made to enhance results.

Only after improvements are made, sometimes requiring multiple cycles of execution, can the organization move to the **Maintain** phase, transitioning responsibility for and integrating the innovation into normal operations.

Context — Where

No two implementations are the same and context is often the reason why. Your implementation can be affected by all kinds of internal factors, such as whether or not other organizational changes are being implemented concurrently, shifts in executive leadership, failure of past change efforts, or the current performance level of the organization. Your implementation can also be shaped by external factors, such as changes in the regulatory or economic climate, actions taken by competitors or partners, or even popular opinion about what you are implementing.

For this reason, you should periodically take stock of your operating environment and incorporate your assessment of contextual risks and opportunities into your decisions and plans. Although it would be convenient, most implementations do not take place in a bubble sealed off from outside influences. So, it's best not to act as if they do.

PART III: WHEN

We start our deep dive into the implementation framework in this section, by looking at phases. Phases are a valuable tool for answering questions about when things will happen and how long things will take in the implementation. In this part, we'll review the five phases of implementation and how to use them to focus your actions at different stages in the implementation. Additionally, we'll discuss how to uses phases as a tool for planning and communication.

Finally, be sure to check out the Appendix, where you'll find a checklist, organized by phase, that you can use to jump-start planning for your next implementation.

FIVE PHASES OF IMPLEMENTATION

Decide, Prepare, Execute, Improve, Maintain

Phases outline critical points in the life cycle of your implementation. They help you to focus your efforts appropriately given where you are in the process. In this chapter, we briefly review the five phases of implementation.

Five Phases of Implementation

In my framework, I use five phases to illustrate how you should adjust the focus of your decisions and actions throughout the life of the implementation.

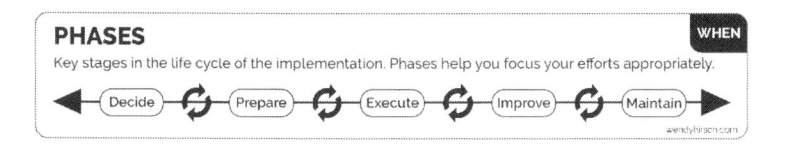

Figure 5 – Phases

Decide

In the first phase, Decide, you lay the foundation for the implementation, clarifying what you are doing and why you are doing it. You define the desired outcomes of the implementation and choose the innovation that will be implemented to achieve those results. Finally, in this stage, you should aim to reach a general agreement on the level of resourcing that will be available for the effort (money, people, time).[1]

Prepare

In the Prepare phase, you develop the infrastructure that will support the implementation. You ensure critical components are in place and roles are filled. You also develop the plan or roadmap that will guide the execution of the implementation.

Execute

In the Execute phase, you start to embed the innovation in your organization, guided by the plan you developed in the previous phase. During execution, you deliver training and coaching as well as gather and monitor progress data to support future improvements.

Improve

In the Improve phase, you review learning from your initial implementation to identify what worked well, and where you need to make adjustments. You plan for refinements you will make in future execution cycles.

Maintain

Once you have fully embedded the innovation in your organization, you need to transition it to normal operations. During the Maintain phase, you finalize who will provide ongoing support and ownership for the innovation and how you will prepare them to take on this role. You also transition staff from the implementation team back to their regular responsibilities, as well as document the implementation to ensure your experiences can inform future efforts at your organization.

Given the iterative nature of implementation — you try something, learn from it, and try again — the first four phases may be revisited several times during the life of the implementation. However, the Maintain phase only happens once.

Phases Support Best Principles

Although I use five phases in my framework, I don't think the specific number or names of the phases are critical. If you think four or six phases would work better for your situation, or want to call them something else, go for it! However, in doing so, I strongly urge you to ensure the three principles outlined below remain true. They are:

1. Implementation is a **multistage and iterative process.** There are more than two phases — start and finish — and you may cycle through some phases more than once.

2. Effective implementation requires **significant effort both before and after the execution** of what you are implementing.

3. You must **proactively transition** the implementation to ongoing operations.

You can use phases to ensure these principles inform your planning and communications. They can be used to clarify and communicate things such as: Where are we now? Where are we headed? What path will we take to get there? And, always a favorite — How long will it take?! In the next chapter, we explore a variety of ways you can use phases to support an effective implementation approach.

Notes

1. Some change management methodologies start only *after* a decision to implement is made. I disagree with this approach. In my view, the decision to change is an integral part of the implementation. It affects everything that comes after it and, as such, should not be treated as a separate process.

PHASES: A VERSATILE AND VALUABLE TOOL

Clarify location, direction, and duration

A city adopts a new approach to drug offenders, slowly

Heavy-handed police tactics used with low-level drug offenders in New Haven, Connecticut, were causing increased alarm in the city. Public outcry against methods perceived as too extreme led a team from the city to search for alternative ways to respond to drug addicts. The team found a promising program in Seattle, Washington, called LEAD. This program empowers police officers to divert drug offenders to treatment, social services, and other programs, rather than arresting them. An independent study found that individuals in the LEAD program were nearly 60% less likely to be rearrested than a control group, in which individuals were arrested instead of being diverted to support programs.

After visiting Seattle to see the program in action, folks in New Haven were excited and ready to go "all in." But those leading the effort advocated for a phased approach. The team opted to undertake a pilot, working intensely with partners in targeted communities to conduct not only the initial effort but also to identify ways to adapt and improve it. The administrator in charge of the effort noted: "There is interest in stakeholders…to scale up LEAD immediately to a city-wide level. We recognize why people would want that. But there's a great lesson to be learned when you start small and learn from the pilot what works and what doesn't work."[1]

Phases are a valuable tool for implementers because they enable you to frame the implementation journey in a way that is relevant to all stakeholders, despite differences in their function, position, or degree of involvement in the effort.

In this section, we review four ways phases can help you to sharpen your implementation approach and build understanding among stakeholders. Specifically, we look at how phases can help provide a shared sense of:

- **Location:** Where are we now? Where are we headed? What happens when?
- **Direction:** How do we get from here to there? Should we expect a straight line or a more circuitous route?
- **Duration:** How long will this take? How fast will we go?
- **Destination:** Where does the journey end? How do we want to finish it?

Location: Where Are We Now? Where Are We Headed?

Phases provide stakeholders with a sense of location by outlining the starting point of the implementation, the endpoint, and stops along the way. Offering some certainty about the process the implementation will follow can allay stakeholder anxieties about the unknown and also help to educate them about how the implementation will play out.

I've found that most people want to start full-scale execution immediately, as we saw in the case outlined at the start of the chapter. They want to show up and go! Who wouldn't? However, implementation research indicates that successful implementers invest adequate time preparing before they execute anything. They clarify the purpose of the implementation, evaluate potential solutions to achieve that purpose, and plan how the chosen solution will be rolled-out and managed.

When people are itching to immediately start "doing stuff," I don't suggest citing research findings, however. Instead, you can use the story of the phases to help explain why that's not the best idea. I often do so using an analogy from a common experience.

For instance, I once had an executive say to me, "I just want to do the execute phase. Can't we skip the rest?" I said, "Let's look at that. What if we think of it in terms of the hike you took last weekend? Did you have to do anything before you started hiking? Like, *decide* which trail you would follow? Maybe *prepare*, by printing out a map and packing water and food. You probably also had to get directions and drive to the trailhead? Yes? This implementation is pretty much like your hiking experience. Right now, we aren't at the trailhead. We are at the house trying to decide what trail to take. We have quite a bit of work to do before we start hiking!"

It's pretty simple stuff, and may even seem a bit hokey. But, it works just about every time!

Direction: Loops Versus Lines

Phases can also help you to educate stakeholders about the route or flow of the implementation. Although implementation is often depicted as a linear process, it rarely is. While you are aiming for a forward progression from start to finish, you should expect to loop back, reassess based on learning, and try again.

In this case, loops are not an indication that something has gone wrong. Instead, they are a way to ensure things go right. Learning is iterative. So, you should anticipate that your implementation journey will have curves and corners, as well as mountains and valleys. It's more like a ride on a roller coaster than a train.

Three options: Try before you buy

The type of ride you'll have depends on how you shape the implementation journey. You can proactively integrate iterations into your approach, from which your team and the organization can learn. There are a variety of ways of doing this, each of which requires different amounts of time, flexibility, and coordination.

You'll likely make final decisions about your roll-out approach during detailed planning. However, I believe you should be aware of your options and have a general sense of the path you'll follow in the early days of the implementation. Why? Because in the absence of information, people will make assumptions. Most often they will assume that full implementation will definitely happen and that everyone will have access to the innovation at the same time. Rather than working to shift such expectations, I recommend you use phases to shape expectations at the outset.

Below, we explore three ways you can integrate planned iterations into your implementation approach.

Pilots

A pilot helps you to understand what it's like to use the innovation in your context by executing it first on a small scale. It's an experiment that allows you to check assumptions, test the solution you are implementing, verify your plans, as well as identify the best approach for embedding the innovation in your organization. However, pilots may not always be feasible.

Pilots can require a fair amount of time and resources to develop and execute. As such, they may be most appropriate for implementations that are likely to have a significant impact on the organization — fundamentally affecting revenues, costs, or core operating procedures.

Second, pilots are usually carried out with the assumption that they may fail. If the pilot reveals the solution is not workable for your context, or the implementation needs a major rethink, a possible outcome is that you pull the plug on the effort. Not all organizations and leaders are comfortable with the flexibility required to do that.

The opposite can also be true. Some organizations get addicted to pilots. They pilot and pilot some more searching for a perfect intervention and never fully commit to one. If you find yourself in either scenario, consider the other options below.

Graduated schedule

A graduated schedule involves starting the implementation with a small set of initial users and expanding from there, learning as you go. Unlike a pilot, when using a graduated schedule you assume that you *will* be implementing the innovation with all intended end users eventually, but that you will evolve through the process.

For example, if you will ultimately implement the innovation with 20 teams across multiple departments, you might start with an initial round of implementation involving one team from each department. You focus on learning — Did it take people longer to catch on than you thought? What obstacles did they encounter? What aspects of the innovation did they love? Hate? Then you adjust your approach and implement with a broader set of end users, and so on. Using a graduated schedule demands time and coordination as well as a degree of organizational patience and flexibility. Should you find those in short supply, consider the last option — testing.

Testing

You can incorporate testing into various aspects of your implementation approach. For example, you can use prototypes, or do a "paper walkthrough" of proposed changes with impacted stakeholders to get their input. You can conduct a dry run of your training with some end users to get their feedback before training everyone. You can test key messages with end users to support clearer communications.

Testing provides opportunities to get feedback from end users about their actual experiences — what they were confused about or challenges they ran into — rather than their opinions or assumptions. Testing is often illuminating, both for the end user and for the implementation team. I argue it should be part of all implementations.

Duration: How Long Will This Take?

As you likely noticed, the options for roll-out discussed above require varying degrees of elapsed time. The choices you make about roll-out will extend or shorten the overall duration of the implementation. Phases can help you to illustrate this and begin to craft shared expectations and agreements about time with stakeholders.

Consider this scenario: Three months into the implementation the chief executive bangs her hand on the table and says, "Why is this taking so long?!" Wide-eyed, the implementation lead responds: "M'am. We've only just started!"

As this uncomfortable example demonstrates, the way we view time is relative and mutable. It can vary not only across national cultures, but also between teams, positions on the organizational hierarchy, and individual personalities. Further complicating matters, most of us fall prey to planning bias; we generally underestimate the time needed to complete tasks.

To combat this, I encourage you to view time as a resource in the same way you would people or monetary support for the effort. "Time is money," as they say. From the get-go, you'll need to develop shared expectations about minimum and maximum duration, and likely negotiate the time resourcing allocated to the effort.

Use data, not assumptions

As you delve into planning, you'll develop a detailed schedule. However, even at the outset of your implementation, you can begin to influence people's notions about the duration of the implementation process, by aligning phases to a general time frame. I suggest you do this based on actual data, not assumptions.

When developing high-level duration estimates for the phases of implementation, draw on various sources, such as organizational calendars, previous experience, and cycle times.

Organizational calendars

Many organizations aim to be quick and agile decision-makers, but in reality, they work on a predictable cycle and at a deliberate pace. Unless the stars align and you have particularly strong leadership support, expect decisions related to your effort to be made in accordance with the organization's planning and budgeting calendar, or strategic decision-making process.

For instance, don't predict decisions in three weeks' time, if the relevant decision-making body only meets once a month and it takes at least two months to get on their calendar. You'll also want to be mindful of the organization's busy seasons as well as major holidays or traditional vacation periods, which can all impact the overall duration of the effort.

Previous experience

Gather lessons internally and externally, directly and from secondary sources about how long it takes to implement the innovation you are considering. Don't assume you'll be able to do it quicker than everyone else unless you have particular, verifiable reasons to back up these assumptions.

Cycle time

The time it takes the organization to realize results from the innovation is often much longer than it takes to put the innovation in place (i.e., to get people to start using it.) You should anticipate needing several execution cycles to achieve full performance. How long this takes will depend, in part, on the innovation you are implementing. If you are implementing something that people will only use periodically, say once or twice per year, the end-to-end duration of the implementation process will be much longer than if you are implementing something people use daily.

However, even if you are implementing something people use daily, you likely won't be able to make strategic improvements that often. You'll need to set a schedule to review learning and identify improvements, perhaps monthly or quarterly. Estimating these cycles times, and how many cycles you'll need before you can transition from implementation to ongoing operations, can help you shape expectations about the full lifespan of the implementation.

Finally, if you want to remain open to piloting or using a graduated schedule as discussed previously, you should account for these in your duration estimates.

Destination: Where Does the Journey End?

Many organizations conclude implementations with the organizational equivalent of the "mic drop." Sometimes endings come simply when the scheduled ending date arrives; sometimes once specific outcomes are achieved. Sometimes files are archived, and lessons learned are conducted, sometimes not. Consultants leave and people go back to their day jobs. Usually, someone finds out at the last minute that she is responsible for the ongoing maintenance of the implemented innovation. Even worse, no one is ever assigned this responsibility and results deteriorate without an apparent owner for the effort.

You can combat the tendency towards abrupt endings just by calling out the existence of the Maintain phase.

In conjunction with the development of desired outcomes at the outset of your effort, you'll want to identify what will trigger the transition to the final phase of the implementation. Will it be based on the completion of a certain number of execution cycles, a specific date, or when particular outcome targets are achieved?

Additionally, if you use phases to frame your detailed planning, you'll be forced to think ahead about the activities required to prepare for and carry out this transition. This can include things such as: Who will be responsible for the effort in the long-term? How will they be prepared for this role? What resources will be transitioned to them? What information or artifacts from the effort will be archived? When will this happen?

Integrating the Framework

In this section, we've discussed how phases can help you frame the journey your organization will take during the implementation. Phases distinguish the significant stages in the implementation, provide a sense of direction, and also help to set expectations about duration and the ultimate destination you are aiming for.

Because phases are like a storyboard for the effort, it can be helpful to think about other aspects of the implementation framework in the context of the phases. For instance, the work you do to support monitoring and measurement will be different during the Define phase than it is in the Execute phase. For this reason, I conclude each of the subsequent chapters with a section that outlines how the focus of the chapter plays out in different phases.

Additionally, to assist you in integrating the various aspects of the framework, I provide an implementation checklist organized by phase in the Appendix. I encourage you to consider the checklist as a first draft; refine it as necessary to meet the context and needs of your effort.

STARTER STEPS: Phases

Phases are a valuable tool for managing expectations and developing shared understanding. To put them to work for you, consider:

1. **Start using phases to frame the implementation ASAP.** You can use the five phases I've outlined or develop your own. Either way, use them consistently throughout the effort to educate stakeholders about the multistage and iterative nature of implementation. The sooner you start creating accurate expectations about the implementation journey, the less time you'll need to spend managing unrealistic expectations and assumptions.

2. **Talk about loops, not lines.** Consider how you will create opportunities for iteration — through pilots, a graduated schedule, or testing — and make sure these are explicit in your visuals and communications about the implementation.

3. **Link phases to a timeline.** Use organizational calendars, cycle times, and previous experience at the outset of your effort to estimate the likely duration of the implementation. You can do this even before you get into detailed planning. People will make assumptions about how long the implementation *should* take if you don't explain how long it likely *will* take and why.

4. **Begin with the end in mind.** For a graceful ending, think in advance about the transition from implementation to ongoing maintenance, including when and how it should happen.

EXPERT TIPS

Less is more. Using phases as a communications tool can help you to take some, not all, of the uncertainty out of the early stages of implementation. Resist the temptation to add too much detail to phase descriptions or to try to answer all potential questions. To be relevant to a diverse body of stakeholders, communications about phases should be relatively high-level.

Uses phases to test expectations and negotiate. Anticipate and welcome discussion about the phases, your duration estimates, and how you plan to build iteration into your effort. You'll need to influence and adapt to leadership and stakeholder expectations. Be sure key decision-makers understand and agree on the key aspects of the journey you've outlined.

Notes

1. This case was adapted from DeShong, T. (2017, October 13). LEAD by example. *The Yale Herald*. Retrieved from https://yale-herald.com/lead-by-example-8645e6251531

PART IV: HOW

In this section, we delve into how you do the work of implementation, through an exploration of the components of the implementation framework. The six components represent the core tools, both tangible and conceptual, that provide structure to your approach and guide your actions. You'll learn what each component is, why it's important, and how to start using it in your organization.

DESIRED OUTCOMES

The vision and rationale for the change

Clear goals support cross-departmental collaboration to save lives

At a San Francisco area children's hospital, doctors noticed that an increasing number of young patients were experiencing kidney damage. This increase was due in part to a rise in multi-drug treatments, with some children receiving 2-3 medications that were known to be toxic to the kidneys (known as nephrotoxic). Extended use of such drugs could result in acute or chronic kidney damage and even death.

Doctors from the nephrology department teamed up with IT to develop a monitoring solution to help identify at-risk children and prompt a conversation with their attending physicians about alternative treatment strategies. The goals of the monitoring program were to eliminate all preventable cases of acute kidney injury and to ensure nephrotoxic medications were only given if needed and then only for the duration required.

For the program to work, the doctors from nephrology needed more than help from IT. They also needed the cooperation of colleagues in the pharmacy, who would use the new monitoring reports built by IT, as well as the clinicians treating the children. To develop a partnership amongst these different parties, the purpose and desired outcomes of the program proved essential.

The IT leader for the effort reflected that his team, as well as the pharmacy team and other clinicians, benefited greatly from the clarity of the purpose and goals of the program. He noted: "Oftentimes when we're doing IT implementations it's easy to forget…to clearly define an outcome and track that outcome. A lot of IT projects are put in…and you're not really sure what the outcome was." Fortunately, that was not the case here. After a year, the program resulted in a decrease in exposure to nephrotoxic medications by nearly 40% and almost a 50% reduction in acute kidney injury. Perhaps most significantly, the effort directly benefited over 200 kids.[1]

Perhaps the most significant questions you will answer in your implementation are these: What do you want to achieve and how will you know you've achieved it?

In this section, we cover how to answer these questions through the development of desired outcomes. These outcomes will serve as the touchstone against which you will calibrate all other decisions in your implementation.

For this reason, I highlight desired outcomes as part of the framework apart from performance measurement and monitoring. Although desired outcomes are related to measurement, their importance is such that they demand to be called out separately.

Put the Horse Before the Cart

Identifying the desired outcomes for a change requires you to articulate the problem you need to address or the opportunity you want to capitalize on through the implementation. However, it is not uncommon for leaders, managers, implementers, and other agents of change to get excited about a solution — what they are going to implement — before they clarify why they are implementing it.

Focusing first on solutions is troublesome because a solution in search of a problem rarely provides value to the organization. It's like putting the cart in front of the horse; it doesn't get you very far. As the leader of the implementation process, you need to direct attention to the right questions at the outset — Why are we doing this and what do we want to achieve?

A Simple Question That May Not be Simple to Answer

Questions about the purpose and objectives of the implementation can be hard to answer. They force people to articulate the future they want to create, how it will be different, and what makes that significant. Some questions you can pose to help define the problem you are trying to solve include:

- What is the challenge or opportunity we want to address?
- Why is this important to us now?
- How does this link to the organization's broader goals or interests?
- By the end of the implementation, what must exist to call it a success?
- How will things be different than they are today?[2]

Desired outcomes should clarify priorities

Desired outcomes help to signal why the implementation is necessary and what it will provide to the organization. At this point in the implementation process, these outcomes should define priorities. (You'll develop more detailed measures later.) To help ensure desired outcomes have a clarifying rather than a muddying effect on your efforts, avoid creating a laundry list. Long lists allow people to avoid making hard choices about what's important to them. You can encourage clear decision-making by limiting the number of outcomes. As a starting point, shoot for three to five.

Desired outcomes should be specific enough to be meaningful

Desired outcomes should be detailed enough to be meaningful, but not so granular that the primary objective is obscured. At a minimum, desired outcomes should help people to visualize the direction you are taking, and the scope and significance of what you are trying to achieve during the implementation.

> *Example: Desired Outcome*
>
> *"Customer service will be better" is probably too broad for a desired outcome. A better bet is something like: "We will see continuous improvement in the major indicators of customer satisfaction throughout the next two years." The latter example specifies the focus of the effort on customer satisfaction, rather than the broad topic of customer service. Additionally, the outcome signals the intention to identify specific indicators to track progress and provides an expectation that improvements will be realized within two years. In later phases of planning, the key indicators and the degree of improvement desired can be outlined in greater detail.*

Getting leaders to devise outcomes at the right level can be tricky. During collaborative discussions about desired outcomes, some people will naturally want a lot of detail. Others will want to focus on broad visionary statements. When facilitating the leadership discussion about outcomes, you'll need to find the middle ground.

To give a bit more detail to general comments, pose questions that drive towards specificity: What does that look like to you? How will you know it when you see it? To bring detailed thinkers up a level, try questions that force people to summarize: How would you write that as a newspaper headline? How would you explain that to your grandfather?

In such discussions, it can also be helpful for participants to define what they *aren't* aiming to achieve through the implementation to sharpen understanding of the scope of the effort.

Developing Outcomes Collaboratively Pays Off

Ensure the right people are involved

When you set out to create a purpose statement and related outcomes, you first need to clarify who should be involved in developing them. In most cases, desired outcomes are best formulated through a collaborative process. Broad collaboration requires more effort than working with a single leader to lay out the objectives of the implementation. However, it can improve the quality of decisions, by ensuring varying perspectives and unique information are considered. It may also strengthen the coalition of support for the change in the long-run. This is particularly important when you are implementing changes that are anticipated to have a significant impact across an organization.

If you haven't yet created a governance body for the implementation, work with the sponsor to identify essential voices who should be part of the discussion on desired outcomes. (If you don't yet have a sponsor — STOP! I advocate against proceeding until one is identified. The sponsor is a critical voice in deciding the outcomes of the effort.)

Three options for facilitation

Once you've decided who will be involved in developing the desired outcomes, you'll want to consider various options for facilitating the discussion about them. You can gather the entire governance body, or relevant leadership group, for a brainstorming and prioritization exercise. However, I often find groups struggle when starting from a blank slate.

To help alleviate this difficulty, you can work with the executive sponsor to develop a draft purpose or problem statement and key outcomes, which you can use to kick off a discussion with the full leadership group. If you do so, you'll need to ensure the sponsor is not too wedded to her ideas. You'll also need to mitigate the risk that the group will simply rubber stamp whatever the sponsor creates.

Another option is to conduct one-on-one interviews with leaders or to survey them to gather initial ideas that can be used to seed a broader discussion on outcomes. Highlighting areas of agreement and disagreement in the information collected is a particularly useful way to focus such a conversation.

Don't skip the process

If you find yourself assigned to an implementation that's already well underway, but hasn't yet articulated desired outcomes, you won't be the first. Take steps to clarify the purpose and desired outcomes as soon as possible. One way of doing this is to summarize what you believe them to be, based on conversations and existing documentation. Then take a draft purpose statement and desired outcomes to the governance body or relevant leadership team for review, adjustment, and approval.

For more on leadership and the roles of the sponsor and governance body, see Part V.

Put Desired Outcomes to Work for You

Throughout the implementation, you'll likely be asked one question more often than any other: Why are we doing this? Don't answer that question differently each time it is asked. Use your desired outcomes to answer it consistently every time — in staff meetings, written communications, training, and even casual conversation. You'll invest a lot of effort into developing your desired outcomes. Be sure to use them.

Phases and Desired Outcomes

Implementation is an iterative process; you probably won't articulate your desired outcomes perfectly the first time around. You should anticipate working on the desired outcomes of the effort throughout the implementation. In the **Decide** phase, aim to develop clear, high-level outcomes. In the **Prepare** stage, you'll get more specific, creating distinct measures and targets related to each outcome.

During the **Execute** phase, you'll gather data and measure progress towards the outcomes. In the **Improve** phase, you may adjust the outcomes in light of learning from your initial experience, before undertaking additional execution cycles. In the **Maintain** phase, you may again modify the desired outcomes, to signal how the organization aims to benefit from the innovation now that it has become part of normal operations.

> **STARTER STEPS: Desired Outcomes**
>
> Desired outcomes help to guide most other decisions made during the implementation. Take care in their development. To get started, you'll want to:
>
> 1. **Identify the leaders whose opinions matter most.** Your first challenge may be ensuring you have the right people involved in conversations about outcomes. Many people will have opinions; you need to sort out whose opinions matter. Work with the sponsor of the effort to identify who must agree to the outcomes.
>
> 2. **Clarify the challenge** or opportunity that the implementation is intended to address. This is ideally done early on in the decision-making process *before* the innovation is identified or the implementation team is secured.
>
> 3. **Clarify the three to five things the implementation must achieve.** Aim for high-level statements that articulate how things will be different if the implementation is successful.
>
> 4. **Document the outputs of these discussions; use the outputs as key messages in your communications.** Create a summary document that includes a simple statement of the challenge you are trying to address and the outcomes you seek. This will act as a guide for decision-making and communications throughout the implementation. It is not uncommon for folks to lose sight of the goals of an effort over time. Therefore, having the desired outcomes documented is an asset you will use repeatedly.
>
> EXPERT TIPS
>
> **Perfection is the enemy of the good.** Work to ensure you have agreement on and a shared understanding of the high-level outcomes; the wording is less important than the meaning. In later phases, you will develop more granular measures and targets.
>
> **Keep outcomes to a minimum.** Focus on top priorities. It's very easy for people to create a laundry list of outcomes to avoid making hard choices. However, such lists dilute attention from what is most important.
>
> **Outcomes must be defined by the organization.** Setting the bar the organization aims to reach through the implementation is an organizational responsibility. As the implementation or project lead, you can't develop the outcomes and sell them to the leaders. The outcomes must come from the organization itself. Resist the urge to fill in the blanks to get things moving...things should not move anywhere until desired outcomes are defined and agreed to by relevant organizational leaders.

Notes

1. This case was adapted from Sutherland, S. and Palma, J. (2017, September 22). Preventing acute kidney injury: NINJA report. [Webinar]. Retrieved from http://www.himss.org/library/lucile-packard-children-s-hospital-stanford-and-stanford-children-s-health-davies-enterprise-award
2. You may also want to consider guidance from researchers at MIT, who suggest a problem statement should be: important and linked to a clear organizational goal; clearly outline the gap between the current and future state; include quantifiable elements; be as neutral as possible related to the causes of the problem; and be sufficiently small in scope that it can be addressed. See Repenning, N., Keifer, D., and Astor, T. (2017). The most underrated skill in management. *MIT Sloan Management Review, 58*(3), 39. Retrieved from http://sloanreview.mit.edu/article/the-most-underrated-skill-in-management/

THE INNOVATION

What you implement

Baby boxes — A simple solution, but is it effective?

In 2017, hospitals in Texas announced they would distribute over 400,000 cardboard baby boxes to new mothers when they left the hospital. (Baby boxes are filled with items for the infant and can also be used as a bassinet.) Aimed at reducing infant sleeping deaths, a similar baby box program was announced by hospitals in Ohio, New Jersey, and Alabama.

The enthusiasm of American hospitals for the boxes seems to have been inspired by their use in Finland, where such boxes have been offered to all new mothers for decades. Moreover, Finland boasts one of the lowest infant mortality rates in the world. But are these boxes the reason?

Some experts doubt the boxes are behind the low infant mortality rate, noting the fact that less than 40% of Finns use the boxes as a sleeping place for their infants. Rather, they say free healthcare and extensive guidance given to new mothers are responsible. Others note Finland's low rates of pre-term birth, which is a leading cause of infant mortality in the United States.

However, some supporters of the boxes point to new research that indicates that such boxes, along with face-to-face instruction, may increase safe sleep practices, specifically reducing bed sharing among mothers and infants. As one researcher noted, "We are of the thought process it can only help." With U.S. hospitals set to provide nearly 20 times as many boxes as are distributed annually in Finland, it seems we are about to find out.[1]

Not even the most talented team can get results from an innovation that is not a good fit for the problem at hand or the context in which they are implementing. When deciding what to implement, it's essential to dig beneath the surface of potential solutions, to understand what they are, how they work, and what it takes to implement them successfully.

In this chapter, we review ways to identify the solution — referred to as the innovation — that best fits your need, organizational culture, and capacity. We also discuss factors to consider when defining and documenting the innovation, which may improve its adoption in your organization.

Assess the Innovation for Fit

There is no unequivocal evidence that indicates an innovation must have certain characteristics or it will fail. However, we can draw some insights from research about the factors that may impact innovation adoption.[2]

Such research indicates that when assessing an innovation, you should look into how well it fits with your organization's need, culture, *and* capacity to implement. To do so, ask questions, such as:

- How relevant is it to the organization's need and desired outcomes?
- How is it demonstrably different or better than current practice?
- What evidence exists to support its effectiveness?
- How clear and easy to use is it?

- How compatible is it with the norms and values of the organization and end users?
- Can it be piloted or tried on a smaller scale?
- Can it be adapted to the organization's context? How?
- How cost-effective is it? Do potential benefits outweigh estimated costs — by how much?
- Is implementation feasible? Does the organization have the required resources and knowledge to implement it or can they be acquired at a reasonable cost?

If your answers to most of the questions above are negative, you may want to keep looking for an alternative innovation to implement. However, if you end your evaluation feeling mostly, but not wholly, positive about the innovation, you may choose to move forward with it, knowing you need to be proactive about managing some barriers to success.

In some cases, you may feel the innovation would work well for your organization, with some adjustments. Research suggests that identifying necessary adaptations before the organization makes a final decision on the innovation is a wise approach.[3] However, you'll want to ensure adaptations do not go so far as to create a different innovation altogether.

Balance Adaptation and Integrity

In any implementation, there will be a natural tension between adhering to a set standard (implementing with integrity) and changing the innovation to fit your environment (adaptation). This tension can exist among those who lead the implementation, particularly when they are trying to resolve resource constraints such as a limited time, funds, or capacity. However, it will also be present among end users who want to modify the innovation to meet their preferences or unique needs.

Implementation is about change, which may feel like a loss of control to end users. When people adapt the innovation to meet their preferences, it can feel like an act of control. It can help create a sense of certainty in a fundamentally uncertain process.

When leading an implementation, your challenge is to find the right balance in the tension between integrity and adaptation. Your goal is *not* to eliminate this tension. In fact, there is some research to suggest adapting innovations to their context may increase their chance of long-term success.[4]

However, adaptation should be undertaken mindfully. Changes that are made for political reasons, or merely to save resources or time, are not likely to lead to higher quality implementation.[5]

Keep the following ideas in mind to help you find the right balance between adaptation and integrity.

Know the difference between a tweak and an adaptation

Any change made to the innovation should be undertaken only after considering its potential impacts. Adaptation refers to modifications made to the innovation, such as:

- Adding or removing content
- Changing how often something is used or delivered
- Changing the means through which the innovation is used or delivered
- Making changes to the innovation to align it with the organization's culture or context[6]

Some modifications may be relatively minor, and won't affect the core components of the innovation.

For example, as part of a global planning effort, I implemented a well-defined group activity to introduce participants to the value of iterative thinking in planning. The exercise was tightly timed and scripted and involved using dry spaghetti to build a tower. The use of spaghetti was not objectionable to most participants but was troubling to those conducting the exercise with colleagues in Africa. They feared the exercise would offend participants because the use of spaghetti as a building material could be viewed as wasting precious food. They tested a variety of other building materials and in the end substituted small plastic sticks for the spaghetti.

They left all other aspects of the exercise the same. This is an example of a cultural adaptation that did not impact the core aspects of the innovation or the desired outcomes.

However, other changes to an innovation can potentially have a significant impact on the results achieved.

Recall the example of the class-size reduction implementation in California. The implementation allowed for school districts to reduce class sizes in only a few grades, or in all classes in grades K-3. Further, what was considered a small classroom in California was much larger than the small classroom in the Tennessee program on which the California effort was modeled. Finally, due to resource constraints in California, uncertified teachers taught many of the new, smaller classes, in physical spaces that were not meant for that purpose. All of these are examples of adaptations that may have reduced the integrity of the innovation.

Understand why and how the innovation works before you change it

Another significant learning from the California case study is that the link between small class sizes and improved student outcomes was not well understood. (We also see this challenge regarding the relationship between baby boxes and infant mortality in the case outlined at the start of this chapter.) In addition to those in California, other school systems adopted the practice without understanding why or how it actually worked.

Subsequently, researchers identified core components of the innovation linked to improved student outcomes. These included not just smaller classes, but also ensuring a robust academic curriculum and teacher training.[7]

Aspects of the innovation that are directly related to the outcomes sought in the implementation are referred to as core components or effectiveness factors.[8] They should not be modified, because doing so may put your outcomes at risk. Effectiveness factors are like the chocolate in a chocolate cake; if you remove the chocolate, you no longer have a chocolate cake.

The challenge for many of us is that we may not be implementing a clearly defined, off-the-shelf practice, tool, or program. Perhaps we are creating the innovation ourselves (such as with a strategy or significant internal initiative), or we are adopting a practice that has not been well-documented by others.

In such cases, it may be hard to *know* what the core components are. Therefore, it is our responsibility to define what we *think* the core components are — based on research, conversations with those who have implemented it previously, and possibly even pilots — and to communicate those clearly and consistently to everyone involved in the implementation.

Even if you are buying a practice, tool, or program from a firm, you'll want to ensure they identify precisely what the effectiveness factors are. Don't assume they know. Be sure to ask.

Engage with stakeholders to identify necessary adaptations

Early engagement with stakeholders can help to support more effective implementation. Such engagement often focuses on how the innovation is implemented, but can also inform the selection of the innovation and related adaptations. End users and other stakeholders may offer unique perspectives you would not have otherwise considered. If you are concerned about the risk of "too many cooks in the kitchen," be explicit about aspects of the effort that will most benefit from their input, and those that are givens and aren't on the table for changes.

Documentation: You Know What It Is, But Do They?

Once you've selected the innovation you will implement, and identified specific adaptations you'll make, you need to document it. Although you may think this is obvious, in my experience failure to adequately document and communicate the innovation is common.

For example, a while back I spoke with a nonprofit executive about the school-based program her organization had created. When program staff went to evaluate outcomes after several years of implementation, they realized they had not identified what made the program, "The Program." They found that their staff, as well as teachers using the program, were adapting it, leaving out components, adding material, and adjusting time frames, in such a way that they were all implementing something slightly different. The standard, non-negotiable aspects of the program were not evident. When I spoke with the executive, the organization was undertaking a major initiative to document the core components of the program as well as to ensure these components were understood and used with integrity by end users, in this case, teachers.

Documentation for your innovation doesn't have to be lengthy or complicated; however, there are a few key pieces you should be sure to include:

Highlight core components, or effectiveness factors, in documentation and training materials. Clarify where and how these components relate to the outcomes or results that you seek. It's important for the team and end users, in particular, to not only understand what the innovation is but also why and how it works.

Clarify the adaptations you have made and why you made them. You'll also want to ensure these adaptations are measured in your evaluation of the implementation. (For more on this topic, see the chapter on Performance Monitoring and Measurement.)

Highlight areas of the innovation where end users, or others, have the discretion to make modifications. When planning, clarify how you'll monitor these changes.

Phases and The Innovation

During the **Decide** phase, you'll use your desired outcomes and problem statement to evaluate potential innovations and select one for implementation. In the **Prepare** phase, you'll document the innovation in detail as well as translate this document into materials used in training and coaching. At this time, you'll also develop the measures you'll use to track the integrity of the innovation throughout the implementation process.

During the **Execute** phase, you'll monitor how the innovation is being used and adopted — How easy or hard is it to adopt? What changes are people making? What parts are people leaving out? What seems to be working well? You'll use this information during the **Improve** phase, to identify adaptations to the innovation that may be necessary to achieve desired results.

In the **Maintain** phase, you'll document the innovation in its revised form and capture learning from the adaptation process that may be useful in the future. In addition, you may want to indicate what types of ongoing updates or revisions to the innovation may be necessary to ensure it remains effective or relevant.

> ## STARTER STEPS: The Innovation
>
> The process of selecting and adapting the innovation you will implement is critical. Take time with it. Remember, this process is often iterative.
>
> 1. **Identify potential innovations and governance.** Be sure you evaluate several potential innovations, not just one, that may address the problem you have identified. Clarify the governance for the decision on the innovation.
>
> 2. **Evaluate each option for fit.** Assess how well each option addresses your organization's need, culture, and capacity to implement. Ensure you understand the core components or effectiveness factors of the innovation, i.e., the aspects of the innovation that are directly linked to the outcomes you seek.
>
> 3. **Make a provisional decision.** Based on your evaluation, identify the best option, or narrow your choices to a smaller set of options.
>
> 4. **Identify adaptations.** Specify any modifications that will be made to the innovation to support greater adoption or improve the fit of the solution to your needs. Ensure adaptations do not impact the core components of the innovation that are linked to the results you seek.
>
> 5. **Make a final decision.** Select the innovation you will implement, including any adaptations that will be present in your implementation. At this stage, the organization may also decide to pilot the innovation, rather than approving a full-scale implementation.
>
> 6. **Document the innovation.** Clarify for stakeholders and end users what the innovation is, how it works, and any areas where they have the discretion to modify it during the implementation.
>
> EXPERT TIPS
>
> **Selecting the innovation may be a relatively simple process or one that is quite involved.** The more novel and impactful the outcomes you seek, the more time and effort you should invest in selecting, adapting, and documenting the innovation you will implement, potentially including a pilot.
>
> **Ensure you identify several viable options.** It's not uncommon for there to be a preferred solution going into the decision-making process. However, research indicates we make better decisions when we consider multiple options, clarify evaluation criteria and fully evaluate the potential challenges involved with each option.[9]
>
> **Engage stakeholders in the innovation selection process, particularly for assistance in identifying potential adaptations.** It's usually the case that end users and other stakeholders can provide novel perspectives that will lead to more informed decision-making.

Notes

1. Case adapted from Peachman, R. R. (2017, May 24). Put your baby in a box? Experts advise caution. *The New York Times.* Retrieved from https://nyti.ms/2qWutnY
2. For example, Wisdom and colleagues reviewed 20 theories and conceptual frameworks to identify attributes of an innovation that may influence its level of adoption. (See Wisdom, J. P., Chor, K. H. B., Hoagwood, K. E., & Horwitz, S. M. (2014) Innovation adoption: A review of theories and constructs. *Administration and Policy in Mental Health, 41*(4), 480-502. doi: 10.1007/s10488-013-0486-4). Karin Guldbrandsson offers a practical discussion and checklist that is mainly focused on innovation selection. It may be particularly relevant for those working in local government. (See Guldbrandsson, K. (2008). From news to everyday use: The difficult art of implementation. *Statens Folkhälsoinstitut, Rapport R* (9). Retrieved from http://www.who.int/management/district/services/FromNewstoEverydayUse.pdf). Finally, through a meta-analysis of 75 studies, Tornatzky and colleagues identified innovation characteristics that may be linked to adoption. (See Tornatzky, L. G., & Klein, K. J. (1982). Innovation characteristics and innovation adoption-implementation: A meta-analysis of findings. *IEEE Transactions on Engineering Management, EM-29*(1), 28-43. doi: 10.1109/TEM.1982.6447463)
3. For instance, see Meyers, D. C., Durlak, J. A., & Wandersman, A. (2012). The quality implementation framework: A synthesis of critical steps in the implementation process. *American Journal of Community Psychology, 50*(3-4), 462-480. doi: 10.1007/s10464-012-9522-x
4. See Greenhalgh, T., Robert, G., Macfarlane, F., Bate, P., & Kyriakidou, O. (2004). Diffusion of innovations in service organizations: Systematic review and recommendations. *Milbank Quarterly, 82*(4), 581-629. doi: 10.1111/j.0887-378X.2004.00325.x and Durlak, J. A., & DuPre, E. P. (2008). Implementation matters: A review of research on the influence of implementation on program outcomes and the factors affecting implementation. *American Journal of Community Psychology, 41*(3-4), 327-350. doi: 10.1007/s10464-008-9165-0
5. See Durlak, J. (2013). The importance of quality implementation for research, practice, and policy. *ASPE Research Brief.* U.S. Department of Health and Human Services. Retrieved from https://aspe.hhs.gov/report/importance-quality-implementa-

tion-research-practice-and-policy

6. See Lee, S. J., Altschul, I., & Mowbray, C. T. (2008). Using planned adaptation to implement evidence-based programs with new populations. *American Journal of Community Psychology, 41*(3-4), 290-303. doi: 10.1007/s10464-008-9160-5

7. See Bohrnstedt, G. W., & Stecher, B. M. (2002). What we have learned about class size reduction in California. Sacramento, CA: California Department of Education. Retrieved from http://www.classize.org/techreport/CSRYear4_final.pdf

8. The term "effectiveness factors" appears in a report by the FrameWorks Institute. In that report, it is defined in this way: "Effectiveness factors…highlight the way that specific features of implementation lead to specific positive outcomes." See Lindland, E., Fond, M., Haydon, A., Volmert, A., & Kendall-Taylor, N. (2015). "Just Do It": Communicating implementation science and practice. A FrameWorks Strategic Report. Washington, DC: FrameWorks Institute. Retrieved from https://www.frameworksinstitute.org/evidence-and-implementation1.html

9. For more on group decision-making see my blog article on the topic. Hirsch, W. (2017, April 21). Want your team to make better decisions? Be sure they do this. [Blog post] Retrieved from http://wendyhirsch.com/blog/team-better-decision-process

PERFORMANCE MONITORING AND MEASUREMENT

How to understand what's working, what's not, and why

Using data to drive results in Pakistani schools

In 2010, the Chief Minister of the Pakistani province of Punjab approved an ambitious roadmap to enhance education in the region. The roadmap included a core set of priorities, among them reducing teacher absenteeism. By 2015, some impressive results from the implementation were reported, including a decrease in teacher absenteeism from 19% to 9%.

At least part of the credit for these results has been attributed to efforts to collect, analyze, and communicate progress data. For example, all schools in the province collected a variety of data and received monthly visits from a monitoring and evaluation team. The team provided technical assistance and captured qualitative information on successful practices. An implementation team supporting the effort analyzed the data to identify areas of strength and weakness. But they didn't keep this information a secret; findings were packaged into visuals that were shared with policymakers as well as the schools themselves.[1]

Successful implementers differentiate between doing and achieving. Achievement sets a higher bar, requiring demonstrable impact in the specific areas targeted by the implementation. In fact, research indicates that the act of setting and monitoring goals is itself linked to performance gains.[2] In other words, monitoring and measuring performance not only helps you to understand if your implementation is having an impact, but it may actually help to make it more impactful!

In this chapter, we'll review how to design and execute the monitoring and measurement component of your implementation. Specifically, we'll look at:

- Leading practices in goal setting and monitoring
- A three-part evaluation framework that can be used in any implementation
- Tips for creating a monitoring and measurement system without getting overwhelmed

The ideas outlined in this chapter should be sufficient to set up a basic monitoring and measurement program for most implementations; however, technical requirements for formal evaluation are not covered as these are beyond the scope of this book.

Some Practices Work Better Than Others

Among the most robust management research available is that investigating the link between goals and performance. When designing your monitoring and measurement approach, you'll be well-served to keep in mind practices that have been found to be effective, such as:

Develop goals that are clear and specific. A goal should indicate the desired result and a time frame for achieving it. In an implementation, this applies to desired outcomes, as well as more specific interim progress measures and targets.

Set challenging, but doable goals. Goals should require hard work to attain. Difficult goals motivate people to put in more effort than easy goals. However, goals should not seem impossible given your staff's current level of skill and knowledge. When goals are too complex or difficult, some research shows they can induce stress and reduce commitment.[3]

Use short-term learning goals when people need to master a new skill, rather than long-term performance goals. Learning goals focus on figuring out *how* to do something. Performance goals focus on *what is achieved* by doing something. In any implementation, you will ultimately focus on a performance goal, but it may take several cycles of execution to get there. During initial execution cycles, shorter-term learning goals may be useful.[4]

Align group and individual goals. Goals have been shown to motivate groups as well as individuals. However, when individual goals conflict with group goals, group performance can suffer. Make an effort to identify and resolve any potential conflicts between the goals of your implementation and those of the business units that may be impacted by the implementation. For example, if the implementation involves a learning curve that may slow sales for a period, but individuals are given bonuses based on sales goals, that could dampen enthusiasm for your effort and reduce adoption.[5]

Communicate the rationale for the goals. Although it's commonly thought that people will work harder towards goals they have a hand in creating, a growing body of research indicates that may not be the case. Participation in goal development does not seem to impact performance. If the rationale behind the goal is clear to those working towards it, that may be enough.[6]

Monitor and share information about progress. Research indicates that checking in on progress and sharing feedback is an important way to motivate people towards a goal. In fact, there is some evidence that when progress is documented and shared publicly, it has a greater impact on achievement.[7]

Your Monitoring and Measurement System

Although some of us may have access to an advanced, technology-enabled mechanism to capture, analyze, and communicate data related to our implementation, many do not. That's ok. In this chapter, I use the term "system" not to refer to information technology per se, but rather the notion of an interconnected set of things that comprise a whole. Regardless of your degree of IT sophistication, you can develop such a system. It just takes thoughtful preparation and some effort.

Such a system has four parts, which we will review in detail below. They are:

1. What you will measure and why — *A simple framework*

2. How you'll measure it — *Goals, measures, and targets*

3. How you'll organize your efforts — *Data collection and management*

4. How you'll use what you learn — *Analysis and action*

1. What you will measure and why – *A simple framework*

Let's return once again to the example of the class-size reduction effort in California. The stated purpose of that effort — the desired outcome — was improved student achievement in reading and math. However, evaluations revealed that although this innovation proved universally popular with teachers and parents, it was expensive and did not consistently impact student achievement.

Was it successful? Well, that depends on how you define success.

I suggest that you think about success in implementation as being multi-dimensional, rather than a singular thing you do or do not attain. In this way, we might view the California case as a partial success. It was well-liked by parents and teachers, which is no small thing. However, it fell short in boosting student achievement.

In her research on the implementation of strategic decisions, Susan Miller, a professor at Durham University in the UK, offers a helpful framework that we can use for evaluating implementation success. It includes three dimensions: completion, achievement, and acceptability.[8] I adapt and summarize these dimensions in Figure 6 and the discussion that follows.

A SIMPLE MEASUREMENT FRAMEWORK
Consider Three Dimensions of Success

COMPLETION
Did you finish the implementation?
Did you complete all the intended aspects of the implementation within the anticipated timeframe?

ACHIEVEMENT
Did you realize your desired outcomes?
How well does the innovation perform? Did you produce the results you intended?

ACCEPTABILITY
Are your stakeholders satisfied?
How pleased are stakeholders with the implementation process and outcomes?

Figure 6 — Measurement Framework

COMPLETION: Did you finish all intended aspects of the implementation?

You can evaluate success related to completion by first comparing what you did with what you intended to do. Assessing completion requires clear documentation of the core components of the implementation, i.e., its non-negotiable aspects. (For more on core components see The Innovation chapter.)

Second, you can evaluate how well you and others managed the implementation, for instance in terms of budget and timely execution. To do so, you must have an implementation plan, which includes a schedule of milestones aligned with a budget. (For more on planning, see the chapter on Infrastructure.)

ACHIEVEMENT: Did you produce your desired outcomes?

In the achievement dimension, you investigate progress made related to your desired outcomes. You measure things such as decreased costs, increased customer satisfaction, reduced infant sleeping deaths, or higher student achievement in reading and math.

Because implementation is rarely a one-and-done endeavor, you should consider developing a graduated set of achievement targets. Doing so helps you to align performance expectations with the current maturity level of the innovation in the organization. Graduated targets might look something like this:

- **Initial:** Documented use of the innovation in X% of teams.
- **Minimally viable:** Documented Y-level performance gains for X% of teams.
- **Full performance:** Desired outcomes achieved.

Using graduated targets can help to rein in unrealistic expectations about how quickly outcomes can be achieved. I feel comfortable saying that 99% of the time it takes longer to see results than most people imagine.

Using graduated targets can also be motivating. As noted in the previous discussion about goal setting research, setting short-term learning goals, in addition to long-term performance goals, can help drive staff to keep working towards a challenging objective.

ACCEPTABILITY: Are your stakeholders satisfied?

In the acceptability dimension, you assess the value stakeholders place on the implementation — were the achievements worth the effort *to them*? Recall the class-size reduction effort, which was incredibly popular with teachers and parents alike. I'm sure their perspectives influenced policymakers and school administrators. Although stakeholder satisfaction is not itself sufficient to indicate the overall success of an implementation, it is a necessary aspect of it.

I don't think it's possible to achieve your desired outcomes if everyone involved in the implementation hates the process or the innovation you are implementing. It's normal and often productive for there to be some level of resistance and skepticism towards a change. Measuring acceptability helps you to understand how well you are responding to such resistance. Your abilities on this dimension will be integral to your long-term success as an implementer.

2. How you'll measure it — *Goals, measures, and targets*

Once you know the outcome areas you want to assess, you need to develop a way to assess them. This involves creating specific goal statements, measures, and targets.

People use these terms differently, so let's briefly review how they are defined in this book. I use "goal" or "goal statement" to refer to what you want to achieve regarding outputs or outcomes (e.g., increased quality). I use "measure" to indicate the data you'll use to evaluate the change (e.g., the number of complaints; the number of corrections; user satisfaction rating). I use "target" to indicate how much change you want to see (e.g., 10% increase from baseline in six months; 15% cumulative improvement from baseline in one year).

When developing goal statements, measures, and targets consider the information on good practices shared previously. Also, you'll want to plan for situations when you don't yet know enough to set targets or have access to the exact data you need for your measures. In such cases, baselines and proxy measures can be useful.

Baseline data

If you don't yet know enough to set realistic performance targets for a particular outcome, resist the temptation to guess. You may grossly miscalculate what's possible, which can impact perceptions of your effort. It can be more productive to forgo targets at first and collect baseline data instead. You can do this during a pilot or your first execution cycle and then use the baseline data to develop targets for subsequent periods.

Proxy measures

You can and will dream up things you want to achieve and measure for which you have no data, or for which data would be too time-consuming or expensive to track. In such cases, you should consider using proxy measures.

Proxy measures are indirect measures. For instance, Gross Domestic Product is a proxy measure for standard of living; murder rate is a proxy for public safety. Proxy measures are often identified by reviewing data that *are* available to you. To make sure you are drawing on all readily available sources of data, consider reaching out to colleagues who may conduct surveys or manage process reporting that can provide data on areas of interest to you. Finally, it's right to be cautious when drawing conclusions from proxy measures. As you use these data, you'll want to continuously evaluate if they are accurate enough for your purposes or if you should look for other sources.

Example: Using Proxy Measures

An organization I know was looking for ways to monitor progress for a new program aimed at improving ethical management practices. How do you measure ethical actions? The organization ended up using two proxy measures for ethical management: the number of internal audit findings and on-time resolution of those findings. These measures were chosen because they were relevant. Before the roll-out of the ethical management program, many audit findings were left unaddressed. Second, the data were accessible. Automated reports that included this information were available, which made tracking this measure relatively easy. Leaders at various levels of the organization reviewed these data quarterly to identify necessary follow-up actions. Providing leaders with access to the data on a regular basis also helped to ensure the ethical management program remained part of ongoing management conversations.

3. How you'll organize your efforts — *Data collection and management*

It takes time and foresight to collect data and format what you collect in a manner that can be easily analyzed and shared. Failure to do so can lead to missed opportunities; you won't get a second chance to capture baseline data or conduct "before" surveys. And if you wait until you want to analyze your data to organize and format them, I guarantee you'll wish you hadn't. Below we'll discuss some tips on how to make sure you stay ahead of the curve.

Plan ahead

Once you have developed your goals, measures, and targets, a helpful next step is to create a monitoring and measurement plan. This plan should include:

- The specific data you will collect
- The source (e.g., report, survey, observation)

- When you'll collect the data (i.e., specific dates)
- Who will do it (e.g., capture, format, analysis)
- How and when the data will be used (e.g., review date and audience)

Figure 7 provides a simple example of a monitoring and measurement plan.

EXAMPLE: Monitoring and Measurement Plan

Desired Outcome 1: Our teams productively collaborate					
Goal Description	Measure & Target	Data Source	Collection Date	Responsible	Review Dates
Increased communication across dependent teams	75% of team members rate communication across teams as "strong" by Q4	Quarterly Pulse Survey	Survey distributed in quarterly cross-team communication	Measurement Lead (Arnie P.)	Quarterly Implementation Data Review; Q4 Governance Council Mtg
	Majority of team leads participate in post-milestone debrief sessions	Attendance taken at debriefs	3 debriefs scheduled to date: March 15; June 17; Sept 09	Project Manager (Janyce F.)	Implementation Team Meetings Monthly; Stakeholders Council: July
Goal Description	Measure & Target	Data Source	Collection Date	Responsible	Review Dates
Goal 2					

Figure 7 – Monitoring and Measurement Plan

As you begin to collect data, you can add columns to the right end of the table to track up-to-date progress information on each measure. Doing so provides you with a current summary of progress to date. This can be quite helpful to ensure when a stakeholder asks "How's it going?" you can answer with more specificity than, "Going great!"

Coordinate and collaborate

Your measurement efforts won't happen in a vacuum. To be effective, you need to align them with other aspects of your implementation. For instance, if your stakeholder management plans require you to provide progress updates to the governance body at certain times, you need to integrate this requirement into your data collection plans. You can't present data that don't exist!

A simple way to ensure you have accounted for dependencies between your measurement efforts and other implementation components is to integrate milestones from your monitoring and measurement plan into your overall implementation plan. (For more on planning, see the Infrastructure chapter.)

Additionally, be mindful of dependencies you may have on processes, programs, or systems that are external to your effort. For instance, you may need to align data capture with specific system dates; perhaps you need to pull a report on the 30th of each month. Further, aim to coordinate your data collection with other change efforts that may impact the same stakeholders.This could mean you collaborate on a survey with another initiative, or leverage system data from another process, rather than creating something new.Such collaborations can build trust with your impacted stakeholders because they demonstrate you care about how your efforts affect their workload.

Establish standards

Developing protocols for organizing and storing data can save you an immense amount of time. For instance, using templates to standardize data collection can support efficient and effective analysis. This is particularly useful when a variety of team members are collecting data separately. For example, it's much easier to draw insights from interview notes if they are formatted and coded similarly by each interviewer.

You should also establish and organize a single, shared space (intranet site, shared drive, or cloud storage solution) to store your measurement data so that they can be quickly accessed and, at the end of the implementation, easily archived.

4. How you'll use what you learn — *Analysis and action*

All the data in the world won't help your implementation unless you use them, which includes analyzing what you collect and incorporating what you discover into your decision-making processes.

What does it mean and why does it matter?

Your analysis should focus on answering the "so what" question. For instance, "What does this tell us about X?" and "Why is that important to Y or Z stakeholders?" I encourage you to be obsessive about linking your analysis to the purpose of the implementation, and the evaluation dimensions discussed previously: completion, achievement, and acceptability. It's relatively easy during analysis to stray off into interesting tangents that may not be useful.

What actions should we take?

Plan to review progress against your goals with various stakeholders on a regular basis. At a minimum, you'll want to integrate progress updates into meetings with your implementation team and governance body. Such discussions should be focused on identifying key lessons or informing decisions, such as adjustments that may need to be made to the approach or innovation.

As your implementation changes in response to your analysis and learning, consider if you need to adjust your monitoring and measurement plan as well. If based on feedback and performance data to date, you decide you need to change a procedure or approach used in your implementation, you may also need to adjust your measurement efforts to reflect that change.

What did we actually do and learn?

Over time, your efforts to collect, analyze, and act on feedback about your implementation will create a strong narrative of learning and growth. Sharing this story of progress with stakeholders is a powerful way to develop shared understanding and pride in what has been accomplished, and reinvigorate stakeholders to tackle remaining challenges. Also, it can contribute to a greater appreciation for the role measurement plays in supporting effective change efforts.

Phases and Performance Monitoring and Measurement

During the **Decide** phase, you'll work with your governance body and others to identify desired outcomes for the effort. These articulate the North Star for your implementation and will inform the development of other aspects of your measurement system. During the **Prepare** phase, you'll develop specific goals, measures, and targets, as well as create your data management plan. During the **Execute** phase, you'll actively collect and analyze data, as well as share what you are learning about progress to date. You may use what you learn to make real-time adjustments.

You'll also use your findings during the **Improve** phase, to identify and recommend significant modifications to the innovation or your implementation approach. Additionally, you may need to adjust your measures and measurement plan. This could involve using baseline data to set targets, updating measures based on learning, or changing your measurement practices. If you are undertaking a final evaluation of the effort, you'll do this after the last execution cycle.

Finally, when transitioning to the **Maintain** phase, you'll need to hand off the data you've collected in a usable format and make recommendations for ongoing monitoring and measurement.

> **STARTER STEPS: Performance Monitoring and Measurement**
>
> Monitoring and measurement are essential to gauge progress during the implementation as well as the ultimate results achieved. To set up a simple monitoring and measurement system to track your effort be sure to:
>
> 1. **Familiarize yourself with good practice** in goal setting and monitoring. This is a well-researched management practice — take advantage!
>
> 2. **Develop a framework** that outlines the outcome areas you will measure, such as completion, achievement, and acceptability. This will help you to focus your measurement efforts on what's truly important and avoid blind spots.
>
> 3. **Develop the system** that you'll use to manage your measurement and monitoring program. This includes what you'll measure, how you'll measure it, how you'll organize your efforts, and how you'll use measures to inform decisions.
>
> 4. **Keep it fresh.** You will likely need to revisit your monitoring and measurement plan throughout your implementation. You can anticipate doing this during the Improve phase, but potentially also in response to learning along the way.
>
> EXPERT TIPS
>
> **Start small and keep it simple.** The best way to fail at measurement is not to do it. However, overly ambitious measurement and monitoring plans can quickly overwhelm you and your team.
>
> **Stay focused.** Ruthlessly ask yourself and your team how your measurement efforts are helping you to understand if your approach is effective and if you are achieving the purpose of the implementation.
>
> **Proactively look for ways to use what you learn.** Make promises about the progress data you will provide and follow through to deliver it. This helps to build trust and to develop expectations for data-informed decision-making. To that end, be sure you sync the schedule of decision-making meetings with data collection plans. You need to make data-informed decisions!

Notes

1. This case was adapted from Acasus. (2014, February 12). The Chief Minister's Roadmap. [Blog post].Retrieved from https://www.acasus.com/insights/2017/8/11/the-chief-ministers-roadmap, and Gold, Jen.(2016, January 19) Delivering Development: Lessons from DFID's implementation units [Blog post]. Retrieved from https://www.instituteforgovernment.org.uk/blog/delivering-development-lessons-dfid%E2%80%99s-implementation-units
2. See Harkin, B., Webb, T. L., Chang, B. P., Prestwich, A., Conner, M., Kellar, I. & Sheeran, P. (2016). Does monitoring goal progress promote goal attainment? A meta-analysis of the experimental evidence. *Psychological Bulletin, 142*(2), 198-229. doi: 10.1037/bul0000025
3. See Gary, M. S., Yang, M. M., Yetton, P. W., & Sterman, J. D. (2017). Stretch Goals and the Distribution of Organizational Performance. *Organization Science, 28*(3), 395-410. doi:10.1287/orsc.2017.1131
4. See Barends, E., Janssen, B., & Velghe, C. (2016). Technical report: Rapid evidence assessment of the research literature on the effect of goal setting on workplace performance (pp. 1-19). London: Chartered Institute of Personnel and Development (CIPD). Retrieved from https://www.cipd.co.uk/Images/rapid-evidence-assessment-of-the-research-literature-on-the-effect-of-goal-setting-on-workplace-performance_tcm18-16903.pdf
5. See Barends, E., Janssen, B., & Velghe, C. (2016). Technical report: Rapid evidence assessment of the research literature on the effect of goal setting on workplace performance (pp. 1-19). London: Chartered Institute of Personnel and Development (CIPD). Retrieved from https://www.cipd.co.uk/Images/rapid-evidence-assessment-of-the-research-literature-on-the-effect-of-goal-setting-on-workplace-performance_tcm18-16903.pdf
6. See Locke, E. A., & Latham, G. P. (2002) Building a practically useful theory of goal setting and task motivation: A 35-year odyssey. *American Psychologist, 57*(9), 705-17. doi: 10.1037/0003-066X.57.9.705
7. See Harkin, B., Webb, T. L., Chang, B. P., Prestwich, A., Conner, M., Kellar, I. & Sheeran, P. (2016). Does monitoring goal progress promote goal attainment? A meta-analysis of the experimental evidence. *Psychological Bulletin, 142*(2), 198-229. doi: 10.1037/bul0000025

8. See Miller, S. (1997). Implementing strategic decisions: Four key success factors. *Organization Studies, 18*(4), 557-602. doi: 10.1177/017084069701800402

TRAINING AND COACHING

Build skills and confidence

Doctors learn to show, not just tell

Two medical students in Grand Rapids, Michigan, are hard at work learning to make quinoa lettuce wraps with spicy peanut sauce. They aren't blowing off steam at an after-hours cooking class. Rather, they are in a course that teaches medical residents how to cook the healthy foods they suggest to their patients. The curriculum is delivered by dieticians and chefs and includes lectures, analysis of case studies, and, of course, cooking and eating! During the cooking portion of each class, instructors circulate to demonstrate techniques and answer questions. Why all this effort?

This course is part of a program that aims to prepare physicians to have more effective conversations with their patients about their food and lifestyle choices. Talking about these topics is vital; evidence shows diet and lifestyle are linked to many types of disease. As one instructor noted, this training helps build physicians' confidence to have these conversations with their patients. They are "not only telling patients they need to eat better but are able to now show them how to eat better."[1]

A variety of research indicates that individuals' perceptions of change are influenced by how confident they are in their relevant skills and capabilities.[2] Put another way, people are influenced by how they answer the question: Do I have what it takes to do this? It's hard to be enthusiastic about something when you have no idea what it is or how to use it. That's why training and coaching are integral to implementation.

In this chapter, we'll review critical factors to consider when developing and executing training and coaching to support your implementation. While you may have access to an experienced instructional designer and coach, it's equally as likely that you won't. Either way, the tips provided in this chapter can help you get started.

The difference between training and coaching

Training helps end users and others prepare to fulfill their roles in the implementation. Training often includes information on what the change or innovation is, why it works, how it will be implemented, as well as instruction on any new skills needed to adopt the innovation. Training may be offered periodically throughout the lifespan of the implementation. Even so, research indicates that training alone may be insufficient to support effective implementation.[3] Training should be combined with coaching.

Coaching refers to technical assistance provided on an ongoing basis to help end users effectively apply skills learned in training.[4] Coaching can improve end users' ability to use the innovation with integrity, as well as help them to overcome practical obstacles they may face.

To better understand the difference between coaching and training, and why both are essential, consider your own experience with professional training. In any given training, you probably received new information via a lecture, and maybe you had the opportunity to practice new skills in the controlled environment of the classroom. Perhaps you left the training feeling excited, confident, and ready to try out what you learned. But as you applied your new learning at the office, you found you were not quite sure how to do "X." Or you realized you didn't know what the trainer meant when she said "Y." Or "Z" just happened, and nobody talked about "Z" during the training! You were left on your own to figure it out. That's training. It's useful to introduce you to new ideas and techniques, but may not entirely prepare you for the reality of using them on the job.

Let's imagine an alternative scenario.

What if, when you returned to the office after an excellent training, you could regularly touch base with someone who had deep experience using the innovation? What if this person was also available to discuss your progress and provide feedback to help you improve and build your confidence? That's coaching; it's ongoing assistance to support your active use of the innovation.

TRAINING

Start by answering four questions

Although the primary purpose of training may be to introduce end users to the technical aspects of the innovation they will adopt, it's also an opportunity to increase their understanding of the purpose of the implementation and their role in its success. When developing your training content, take care to answer critical questions most end users have; we review four common questions below.

1. Why are we doing this?

The desired outcomes and organizational rationale for the implementation should be presented upfront during training. Some research indicates that it's important for practitioners and managers to have a shared understanding of the meaning and purpose of the implementation.[5] For this reason, you'll likely review the purpose and objectives of the implementation again…and again…and again to ensure everyone has similar perceptions about these critical components of the effort.

2. What is the innovation and how does it work?

Reviewing the core components, or effectiveness factors, of the innovation helps end users understand how it works. Effectiveness factors are the aspects of the innovation that are linked to the results you desire. (For more on this topic, see The Innovation chapter.) A brief review of the relevant theory underlying the innovation is usually time well spent.

3. How do we do it?

Training at its heart involves teaching the core skills that people need in order to use the innovation with integrity. These may include technical, as well as behavioral, or interpersonal capabilities. Preparing people to effectively use a change may also require you to think beyond the knowledge they may need, to also address conflicting beliefs or resource constraints. These other factors may inhibit the adoption of a change — even when end users have the necessary knowledge and awareness.[6]

4. What's next?

Training should also include a summary of key dates and activities in which training participants will be involved as part of the roll-out of the innovation. Such content can help to lessen end users' uncertainty about what's ahead by offering concrete actions and time frames on which to focus. Providing such information is easy if you have a clear implementation plan. (For more on planning, see the chapter on Infrastructure.)

Clarify learning objectives and use them to evaluate success

Before you start creating training content, you should specify what you want participants to learn during the training, also known as learning objectives. These may relate to the critical questions discussed previously, as well as additional technical content. Learning objectives are often phrased in a statement, such as: "By the end of this training, you will understand A, B, and C and be able to perform, X, Y, and Z." Creating learning objectives helps you to develop training content that is both relevant and sufficient to achieve the purpose of the training.

You can also use learning objectives to ascertain the effectiveness of your training by integrating the objectives into pre-tests and post-training evaluations.

To design for your audience, know your audience

When developing training content, consider not only what you want to teach, but also who you are teaching. It's a good idea to assess the skills and experience of likely training participants to inform your training design. Appropriate instruction for relatively experienced staff may not work well with those who are new to their roles or who have no previous background in the innovation you are implementing.

When conducting a pre-training assessment, ask potential participants what they want to get from the training. This will likely dovetail with your intentions; however, direct input from participants can help you to decide where to place greater emphasis, or what topics to address upfront.

Use a variety of instructional methods

Research indicates that using diverse instructional methods may lead to better training outcomes. As such, aim to go beyond PowerPoint and use a variety of approaches while training. These may include presenting information, demonstrating techniques, and providing participants with opportunities to practice new skills or behaviors.[7]

Practice makes perfect

Training is not merely about information transfer and skill building; it is also an integral part of trust building between the implementation team and end users. Therefore, you should be confident in the material and your methods before launching the training. I recommend conducting a pilot with a subset of the staff who will receive the final training. Doing so will provide you with invaluable feedback that you can use to improve your content and delivery.

Keep in mind that a pilot is geared to help you test the effectiveness of the training — not to learn your lines. Deliver this pilot session only after you have refined the training through several dry-runs with your implementation team.

Let constraints spur your creativity

In a perfect world, we implement in organizational environments that offer excellent facilities and where everyone loves professional development, makes time for it, and fully participates.

The real world is often quite different, presenting challenges related to the availability of time and physical space, as well as low participant interest. While you can't work miracles, you can minimize obstacles by getting creative.

For example, if you can only negotiate two hours of in-class time with a group, but you feel you need four hours of instructional time, can you deliver additional training via the web or an e-learning? Can you set your training offerings apart by providing more inventive activities? Or by holding them in an attractive location? Can you help participants with busy schedules by offering sessions on a variety of dates and times or providing a free meal before or after the training?

Of course, not all challenges can be minimized. Be sure to articulate non-negotiable requirements for participation in training and partner with your implementation's leadership to ensure they are respected. In my experience, establishing expectations for mandatory participation in training is essential to create a baseline of understanding and skills among end users.

COACHING

Why have we never done this before?

Most people recognize the importance of training, but overlook the influential contributions that coaching can make to the success of an implementation. This may be because skill-based coaching is still relatively rare in organizations; we often don't think about things we haven't experienced.

Coaching may also seem daunting to implementers because it is less controlled than training. In training, we provide standard content to a group at specific points in time. Coaching requires ongoing interaction with participants, and thus more coordination and resourcing, as well as different skills than training.

However, the extra effort is worthwhile. Having an experienced partner to help end users overcome roadblocks and avoid rookie mistakes can make a significant difference to the overall results achieved in an implementation.

While research in this area is nascent, we can glean a few promising practices from what is currently available.[8] Even if you are not able to fully resource a coaching approach, you should be aware of these practices and strive to incorporate them into your implementation as much as possible.

Coaching should be formalized, rather than provided on an as-needed basis

Coaching should be provided by a person with experience in the technical aspects of the innovation being implemented. However, in addition to knowledge of the innovation, the coach should also be aware of the basics of the coaching process. For instance, the coach and coachee(s) should specify the format, frequency, and focus of coaching sessions at the start of the coaching relationship. As part of this process, it can be helpful to clarify the boundaries of the coaching discussions. Such boundaries can include the types of topics discussed during coaching, as well as the information that will or will not be shared with others (e.g., supervisors, members of the implementation team, etc.). It can be helpful to outline this in a written agreement between the coach and coachee(s).

You'll also need to consider who will receive coaching, based on their roles as well as your capacity. For instance, it may make sense to target supervisors who are overseeing adoption among end users in their departments. Or you might find group coaching works well for a small set of managers or end users. For some highly targeted implementations, you may provide coaching to all end users.

To select who will receive coaching, consider who is best positioned to amplify its benefits. For example, when I led the implementation of a formal project management method in one organization, I provided ongoing coaching to all 10 project managers involved in adopting the practice. In contrast, participants in training were drawn from a broader group; in addition to project managers, training was available to any interested members of impacted project teams.

Focus on skill development as well as troubleshooting

Coaching in reaction to an obvious problem may not be as effective as proactive coaching that aims to enhance the practitioner's skills, as well as troubleshoot issues. Frame coaching as a means of deepening and sharpening the capabilities of those using the innovation. Doing so may help to ensure coaching is expected on a regular basis, not only when challenges exist.

Seek feedback from a variety of sources

To inform the coaching process, it can be useful for a coach to gather information beyond that provided by the person being coached. For instance, coaches can observe end users while they are using the innovation. The coach may also draw on feedback provided by customers, clients, supervisors, or other staff. The coach can also use findings from monitoring and measurement efforts to inform discussions with the coachee.[9]

Phases and Training and Coaching

During the **Decide** phase, you'll negotiate time and monetary resources necessary to support your coaching and training needs. If you anticipate contracting outside expertise to support this component of the implementation take into account the additional time and expenses required. In the **Prepare** phase, you'll develop your training and coaching approach as well as the content and instructional materials you'll use to support it. You'll also integrate the training and coaching schedule into your overall implementation plan.

During the **Execute** phase, you'll deliver training as well as ongoing coaching. In the **Improve** phase, you'll update your materials and methods based on feedback from training evaluations, coaching observations, as well as monitoring and measurement efforts. You may also provide refresher training with updated content as part of additional execution cycles.

To prepare for the transition to the **Maintain** phase, you will identify ongoing training needs and ensure that all training materials are updated to align with the latest versions of the innovation.

STARTER STEPS: Training and Coaching

Both training and coaching are essential to help end users successfully adopt the innovation being implemented. When developing your training and coaching approach, be sure to:

1. **Articulate learning objectives for training.** Ensure all training content aligns with one or more of these objectives. Develop post-training evaluations that measure the attainment of the objectives.

2. **Undertake a pre-training survey of participants.** This survey will help you to develop appropriate training content for participants' current skill level, as well as to explicitly address their most burning questions.

3. **Ensure training content covers four key areas.** These areas include why you are undertaking the implementation, what the innovation is and how it works, skills end users need to use the innovation effectively, and timelines and next steps.

4. **Develop and execute a structured coaching approach** that includes a minimum set of pre-scheduled coaching sessions, focused on enhancing skills not just reacting to challenges.

EXPERT TIPS

Make choices. Practice. Two pitfalls of training are trying to cover too much material and not preparing in advance. Focus on the highest priority content and practice to build your ability to deliver it well.

Variety is the spice of life, as well as coaching and training! Be sure coaching is informed by feedback from a variety of sources, including the coaching participant, objective data, and customer/supervisor feedback. Use a variety of instructional methods in training, including presenting information, demonstrating techniques, and providing participants with opportunities to practice new skills or behaviors.

Set expectations for participation. People can't learn from training and coaching if they don't attend it. Clarify minimum requirements for participation upfront and leverage leadership to ensure commitments are kept.

Notes

1. This case was adapted from Scott, M. (2017, October 3). Why Spectrum Health is teaching doctors about nutrition, cooking. Retrieved from http://www.mlive.com/news/grand-rapids/index.ssf/2017/10/how_spectrum_health_teaching_r.html
2. See, for example, Erwin, D. G., & Garman, A. N. (2010). Resistance to organizational change: Linking research and practice. *Leadership & Organization Development Journal, 31*(1), 39-56. doi:10.1108/01437731011010371
3. See, for example, Kelly, J. A., Somlai, A. M., DiFranceisco, W. J., Otto-Salaj, L. L., McAuliffe, T. L., Hackl, K. L., ... & Rompa, D. (2000). Bridging the gap between the science and service of HIV prevention: transferring effective research-based HIV prevention interventions to community AIDS service providers. *American Journal of Public Health, 90*(7), 1082. Retrieved from https://www.ncbi.nlm.nih.gov/pmc/articles/PMC1446305/
4. Coaching in implementation is conceptualized differently than it is in other domains. For instance, life coaching or professional coaching may not include the provision of technical assistance.
5. See Greenhalgh, T., Robert, G., Macfarlane, F., Bate, P., & Kyriakidou, O. (2004). Diffusion of innovations in service organizations: Systematic review and recommendations. *The Milbank Quarterly, 82*(4), 581-629. doi:10.1111/j.0887-378X.2004.00325.x
6. For more, see the discussion of the AMO framework in Stouten, J., Rousseau, D., & De Cremer, D. (2018). Successful organizational change: Integrating the management practice and scholarly literatures. *Academy of Management Annals,* 12(2), 752-788. doi: 10.5465/annals.2016.0095
7. For an in-depth discussion and training preparation checklist, see Salas, E., Tannenbaum, S. I., Kraiger, K., & Smith-Jentsch, K. A. (2012). The science of training and development in organizations: What matters in practice. *Psychological Science in the Public Interest, 13*(2), 74-101. doi:10.1177/1529100612436661. For a discussion of training and implementation, see Wandersman, A., Duffy, J., Flaspohler, P., Noonan, R., Lubell, K., Stillman, L. & Saul, J. (2008). Bridging the gap between prevention research and practice: The interactive systems framework for dissemination and implementation. *American Journal of Community Psychology, 41*(3-4), 171-181. doi:10.1007/s10464-008-9174-z.
8. For a discussion on coaching and technical assistance in implemen-

tation, see, for example, Bertram, R. M., Blase, K. A., & Fixsen, D. L. (2015). Improving programs and outcomes: Implementation frameworks and organization change. *Research on Social Work Practice, 25,* 477- 487. doi:10.1177/1049731514537687; Wandersman, A., Chien, V. H., & Katz, J. (2012).Toward an evidence-based system for innovation support for implementing innovations with quality: Tools, training, technical assistance, and quality assurance/quality improvement. *American Journal of Community Psychology, 50*(3-4), 445-459. doi:10.1007/s10464-012-9509-7; and Meyers, D. C., Durlak, J. A., & Wandersman, A. (2012). The quality implementation framework: A synthesis of critical steps in the implementation process. *American Journal of Community Psychology, 50*(3-4), 462-480. doi:10.1007/s10464-012-9522-x

9. For a discussion on how to hold effective debriefs with groups and individuals, see Tannenbaum, S. I., & Cerasoli, C. P. (2013). Do team and individual debriefs enhance performance? A meta-analysis. *Human Factors, 55*(1), 231-245. doi:10.1177/0018720812448394

INFRASTRUCTURE

Physical, administrative, and project management supports

An effective solution, ineffectively implemented

Across the world, millions of people are at risk of infection from lymphatic filariasis, also known as elephantiasis. It's a parasitic disease that leads to the enlargement of body parts, causing severe pain, disability, and social isolation. The good news is, this illness can be eliminated by regularly providing preventative medications to all persons in a particular location for five years. Sounds simple enough. But is it? One review of a medication distribution program in India highlights the challenges.

The goal of this program was to reach 80% of the population in one district with the drugs, every year for five years. However, the program had only given drugs to a little over 30% of the people in the area. Sometimes drug availability was the issue. Distribution campaigns would be planned, and then postponed, sometimes for weeks, because the drugs had not yet arrived. When drugs were available they weren't always taken by those who received them. This was often because the people hadn't eaten recently; the medication should be taken with food. So, they were left with the pills to take later…and they never took them.

Other people were suspicious of the drugs or fearful of potential side-effects, which made them reluctant to take the pills. Finally, some community members were simply not around during the initial round of distribution. If the team didn't return at a later date to provide drugs to these people, they remained untreated.

To improve the distribution effort would require a myriad of efforts, which, when combined, would strengthen the overall infrastructure supporting the implementation. Such improvements could include better planning of drug shipments and monitoring drug availability to ensure timely distribution campaigns, improved training and supervision of drug distributors to increase the number of people actually swallowing the pills, and enhanced communication efforts to reduce resistance by educating community members about the benefits and safety of the drugs.[1]

As you learn more about the implementation framework on which this book is based, you may wonder how to coordinate between its various parts, to avoid working at cross-purposes or having something fall through the cracks. That's a valid concern, and the part of the framework that we discuss in this chapter — infrastructure — will help you to mitigate such risks.

Infrastructure encompasses a variety of enablers

The Oxford English Dictionary defines infrastructure as: "The basic physical and organizational structures and facilities...needed for the operation of a society or enterprise..." I think of implementation infrastructure similarly, as the various enablers — physical, administrative, and project management — needed for the smooth operation of the implementation.

As you read this section, keep in mind that some of these enablers will exist on every implementation, such as those related to project management. However, others will vary depending on the context in which you are implementing. For example, not all implementations will require robust technology supports.

Finally, some elements of the framework discussed in other chapters could be viewed as part of the implementation infrastructure, such as the implementation team or monitoring and measurement. I treat them as distinct aspects of the framework because I feel they should be explored in greater detail. However, it's also correct to think of them as part of the infrastructure through which you support and coordinate the implementation.

Physical Infrastructure

You will undoubtedly require physical resources of some kind to support your implementation. This could include the space in which your implementation team or others will work, tools or other supplies that are required to enable end users to effectively adopt the innovation, or technology to facilitate data management and analysis.

It is best to assess requirements and secure these physical resources upfront. Resist the temptation to figure it out later. That's often a recipe for headaches that can last throughout the implementation.

Think back to the example of the class-size reduction effort in California that we reviewed at the start of the book. When the number of students in each classroom was reduced, it resulted in the need for more physical classroom space. However, there were no advanced plans for additional classrooms. As a result, classes were held in libraries, gyms, and hallways, which were not ideal learning environments.

The lesson from this case is to assess significant physical infrastructure requirements as part of the evaluation and decision-making process related to your choice of innovation. (For more on this topic, see The Innovation chapter).

Administrative Infrastructure

Administrative infrastructure includes organizational policies, practices, or procedures that support the work of the implementation team or the adoption of the innovation. A particularly important component of administrative infrastructure is governance.

Governance

Governance refers to decision-making roles and processes. Governance for your implementation will likely comprise decision-making at many different organizational levels. Decision-makers may include the board or executive team, a governance body specific to the implementation, the executive sponsor of the implementation, the implementation team, as well as individual end users or managers.

One of the project management enablers you'll develop is a governance framework. We'll discuss that later in this chapter, as well as in the chapter on Leadership.

Other administrative supports

Organizational policies or programs can also support the implementation. For example, HR policies, such as flextime, overtime, or rewards programs, can guide how you manage the additional staff effort that may be required during the implementation. Additionally, a formalized internal communications infrastructure such as a newsletter, Lunch and Learn series, or all staff meetings can be leveraged to support your stakeholder engagement efforts.

As much as possible, identify existing administrative supports that you can use, rather than starting off by developing your own. This not only reduces your workload but also better integrates your efforts into the fabric of the organization.

Project Management Infrastructure

If we think of the physical and administrative infrastructure like the spine of the implementation, supporting its weight and providing stability, then the project management infrastructure is like the spinal cord, ensuring coordination of messages between the body and the brain.

In this section, we'll briefly review core parts of the project management infrastructure required to effectively run an implementation. Although project management is a core competency for all implementers, a comprehensive discussion of the topic is beyond the scope of this book. Therefore, if project management is a growth area for you, I recommend studying additional references or taking a course that is aligned with a recognized project management methodology.

The Implementation Plan

Perhaps the most critical aspect of the project management infrastructure is the implementation plan. This plan will differ in scale and complexity depending on the type and size of your implementation. However, every implementation should have a plan. When thinking about your implementation plan, it's also important to understand that it usually isn't a single thing. Rather it's a collection of plans each focused on different aspects of the effort. The implementation plan brings these various plans together in one place.

The source document for your implementation

Your team should view the implementation plan as *the* source document for answers to fundamental questions about the implementation. As circumstances change, you will update it. It is a living document and for this reason version control can be an issue. You can manage this challenge by maintaining a single copy at all times.

Key elements of the implementation plan

Although the details of your implementation plan will differ, such plans generally answer key questions about the implementation, including those discussed below.

WHY?

The purpose and aims of the effort — why you are doing it — will be clarified as part of your work during the Decide phase. Your implementation plan should include a summary of the decisions made during this phase, including a **problem or purpose statement**, as well as the **desired outcomes** of the effort.

WHAT?

A high-level **scope statement** specifies the innovation you will implement. It clarifies both what you will and won't be doing in broad terms. More detailed descriptions of the activities that will be undertaken during the implementation are outlined in a **task list**. In project management parlance this task list is known as a work breakdown structure.

In developing the task list, you'll need to make two decisions upfront — how you'll structure it and the level of detail that you'll include. I recommend using the five implementation phases to structure the task list (as well as the schedule and budget). Doing so will help to ensure you plan for the full lifespan of the implementation.

In terms of the level of detail to include, I recommend trying to have your cake and eat it too. Those responsible for different segments of your effort — for example, training or measurement — may require a more detailed task breakdown than that needed by the implementation lead or full team. As such, you may find it useful to develop a task list with milestones or deliverables at one level, and a detailed list of supporting tasks bundled under it. (For an example, see Figure 8.)

EXAMPLE: Milestones Only

	Start	End	Responsible	Budget
1. Decide				
1.1. Executive Sponsor On Board	2/1/16	3/15/16	Team Lead	$0
1.2. Purpose & Desired Outcomes Approved	4/1/16	6/1/16	Team Lead	$0
1.3. High-level Resourcing Agreement Secured	5/25/16	5/25/16	Team Lead	$0
2. Prepare				

EXAMPLE: Milestones and Detail

	Start	End	Responsible	Budget
1. Decide				
1.1. Executive Sponsor On Board	2/1/16	3/15/16	Team Lead	$0
1.1.a. Sponsor Secured	2/1/16	2/28/16	Team Lead	$0
1.1.b. Sponsor Meetings on Norms	3/1/16	3/20/16	Project Mgr	$0
1.2. Purpose & Desired Outcomes Approved	4/1/16	6/1/16	Team Lead	$0
1.2.a. Leadership Interviews Complete	4/1/16	4/15/16	Project Mgr	$0
1.2.b. Leadership Discussion	4/25/16	4/25/16	Sponsor	$0
1.2.c. Review and Approval	5/25/16	5/25/16	Team Lead	$0
1.3. High-level Resourcing Agreement Secured	5/25/16	5/25/16	Team Lead	$0
2. Prepare				

wendyhirsch.com

Figure 8 – Plan Examples

This tact provides task leaders with the detail they need to execute while allowing the implementation lead to focus on milestones and potential roadblocks. Many project management software packages provide functionality that supports such multi-level planning.

WHEN?

A **schedule** specifies when deliverables, milestones, and tasks will be completed, taking into account dependencies between major milestones. When scheduling, keep in mind that most of us underestimate how long it takes to complete work. To more accurately gauge time requirements consult the actual schedules of similar efforts, or consider adding a standard 5%-10% contingency to all estimates.

Finally, keep in mind that one means of measuring implementation performance is adherence to a schedule, i.e., did you complete the implementation on time? If you need to adjust your schedule during the later phases of the effort, it's good practice to save your original schedule as a baseline. Doing so makes it possible to learn how well your planning assumptions lined up to reality. This learning can also support more accurate planning in future efforts.

HOW MUCH?

Your **budget** will outline the resources available to support your implementation, as well as how they align with your schedule and tasks. An excellent way to create more insightful interim progress reports, and save yourself time, is to develop a budget based on project milestones or deliverables. That way you'll be able to track if your spend rate is aligned with your productivity. For example, if by date X, you've spent 60% of your budget, but have only completed 40% of the planned tasks for that period, you may have some issues.

WHO DOES?

The tasks you outlined in your task list, or work breakdown structure, should all be **assigned** to specific roles on the implementation team, or in the organization. Aligning responsibilities to roles, rather than only to individuals, can help to bring stability to the effort when staffing changes happen. (For more on team stability, see the Implementation Team chapter.) Of course, you may also indicate in the plan the individual who holds this role, to ensure responsibilities are clear and to help balance the workload of individual team members.

WHO DECIDES?

A **governance framework** outlines who makes which decisions for your implementation. For an example, see Figure 9.

When developing this framework start small. Include major types of decisions, not all possible decisions. It's also wise to consider who has the most relevant knowledge and experience to inform certain decisions. For example, the governing council may be well-suited to make strategic decisions on purpose and resourcing, but may not have the expertise needed to identify the best implementation approach. For more information on governance, see the Leadership chapter.

EXAMPLE: Governance Framework

Decision	Decision-Maker	Input	Inform
Desired Outcomes	Governance Council	Executive Team and Division Managers	Implementation Team
Innovation	Governance Council	Implementation Team	Executive Team
Resources	Governance Council	Implementation Team and Executive Team	Division Managers
Schedule	Governance Council	Implementation Team	Executive Team and Division Managers
Implementation Approach	Implementation Lead	Implementation Team	Governance Council
Communications	Communications Lead	Implementation Team	Governance Council
Training Approach	Training Lead	Implementation Team	Governance Council
Measurement and Monitoring	Measurement Lead	Implementation Team	Governance Council

wendyhirsch.com

Figure 9 – Governance Framework

WHO KNOWS?

Two-way communication and feedback are the lifeblood of effective implementation. When developing a **communication plan**, aim for quality rather than quantity. I have rarely found multi-page communication or engagement plans to be useful. A simple grid with columns for who (messenger), what (key messages), when (date), and how (method) is often sufficient.

Integrating communication milestones into the task list and schedule of your project plan can also help to ensure engagement is not seen as an "add-on" but an integral part of your effort. As noted previously, if your organization has an existing communications infrastructure, leverage it as much as possible. (See the Communication chapter for more on change communication.)

WHAT IF?

Particularly on larger efforts, you may have a **risk or issue management plan** that outlines key risks you have identified, mitigation tactics for minimizing them, and triggers for when you should enact contingencies or alternative plans.

To identify potential risks, you may consider holding a pre-mortem with your team and key stakeholders.[2] This method involves facilitating a discussion about failure — you begin by asking the group to imagine themselves in a future where the implementation has failed completely. You then facilitate a brainstorming session to surface the reasons for the failure. The outputs of the discussion can be used to improve risk planning, as well as planning in general.

Supports for a high-functioning team

The project management infrastructure should also support the operation of the implementation team. Be sure to establish clear roles and responsibilities, group norms, and standardized processes to support coordination and communication across the team. They make a difference. For more on this topic, see the Implementation Team chapter.

The Role of Context

All organizations have their own rules, requirements, and expectations. If you are new to the organization, team, culture, or industry you are implementing within, you'd be wise to find an old hand, or even better a few, who can help you to navigate this new territory. Trust them more than your instincts when it comes to context-specific matters until you have your bearings. Such people can help you to identify requirements you would never have thought of, as well as to properly determine the aspects of the infrastructure that are "nice to haves" versus "must haves."

Even if you are familiar with an organization, or team, keep in mind that the further you are from the day-to-day experience of those who will be using the infrastructure you develop, the less accurate your judgment will be on these matters. I advise you to determine infrastructure requirements with the input and counsel of those who will be using these enablers to carry out their work. (Having a diverse implementation team can also help to mitigate such risks. See the Implementation Team chapter for a full discussion.)

Phases and Infrastructure

During the **Decide** phase, as part of the innovation selection process, you will evaluate the infrastructure requirements of various innovation options. You will also secure resourcing commitments from leadership, which should include support for the infrastructure necessary to carry out the implementation. During the **Plan** phase, you will put the infrastructure in place. You'll develop, consolidate, and integrate various planning documents, and establish the norms and processes that the implementation team will use.

During the **Execute** phase, you'll use your implementation plan to guide your team's actions, and identify issues or faulty assumptions that should be addressed. Plan updates may be made immediately, or during the **Improve** phase if large-scale replanning is required.

In the **Maintain** phase, you'll document the infrastructure used to support the implementation as well as your learning about its sufficiency. You may transition some parts of the infrastructure to the team that will provide ongoing operational support for innovation, or archive it to inform future implementation efforts.

STARTER STEPS: Infrastructure

Infrastructure consists of various elements — physical, administrative, and project management — through which you support and coordinate people and activity during the implementation. To develop the infrastructure for your implementation, consider doing the following:

1. **Identify the physical and administrative supports** required to be effective. Include these in your assessment and selection of the innovation you will implement.

2. **Leverage documentation from the Decide phase to inform the development of various project management supports.** Decisions made at the outset of your implementation will provide the boundaries of scope, time frame, and resources necessary to focus more detailed planning.

3. **Set standards for the structure and level of detail that will be included in your plans, schedule, and budget.** Clarifying such standards upfront can streamline planning efforts by focusing team discussions on the content of the plan, rather than debating how it should be organized.

4. **Iterate.** Expect to go through several rounds of planning. With each iteration, identify dependencies and resolve conflicts. If you use a "divide and conquer" method of planning, with various component leads developing detailed plans independently, be sure to hold reconciliation sessions to integrate the plans into a comprehensive whole.

EXPERT TIPS

Uses phases and milestones to organize your plan, schedule, and budget rather than task areas or sub-teams. This can help to ensure you develop a truly integrated plan that addresses all stages of the implementation. It can also streamline progress reporting.

Be aware; you can plan too little and too much. A general rule of thumb is to spend 20-30% of the overall project duration planning. However, the experience level of your team, the novelty of your implementation, and the degree of uncertainty around the project can all impact the length of time required. If the task of planning seems daunting, break it down into bite-size chunks, focused on answering key questions, rather than viewing planning as one huge task.[3]

Notes

1. This case was adapted from Ranganath, B. G. (2010). Coverage survey for assessing mass drug administration against lymphatic filariasis in Gulbarga district, Karnataka, India. *Journal of Vector Borne Diseases*, *47*(1), 61-64. Retrieved from https://www.ncbi.nlm.nih.gov/pubmed/20231778
2. For a detailed discussion of the premortem method, see Klein, G. (2007). Performing a project premortem. *Harvard Business Review*, *85*(9), 18-19. Retrieved from https://hbr.org/2007/09performing-a-project-premortem/
3. See Choo, A. S. (2014). Defining problems fast and slow: The U-shaped effect of problem definition time on project duration. *Production and Operations Management*, *23*(8), 1462-1479. doi: 10.1111/poms.12219, and Serrador, P., & Turner, R. (2015). What is enough planning? Results from a global quantitative study. *IEEE Transactions on Engineering Management*, *62*(4), 462-474. doi: 10.1109/TEM.2015.2448059

COMMUNICATION

The exchange of information and ideas

Can one email make or break an organizational change?

In October 2018, AbeBooks, a marketplace for antiquarian books, sent an email to booksellers in several countries.

The message?

> "Effective November 30, 2018, AbeBooks will no longer support sellers located in certain countries. Your business is located in one of the affected countries and your AbeBooks seller account will be closed on November 30, 2018. We apologize for this inconvenience."[1]

Most likely, the staff at AbeBooks didn't anticipate that this email would set off a worldwide strike amongst its vendors and become a global news story…in the span of just a few weeks.

What happened?

AbeBooks provides a marketplace for sellers of rare and antique books. With this email, the company cut off access to this marketplace for vendors in several countries, with no explanation and very little notice. Although impacted vendors and the membership association that represented them tried to get further information, the company was reportedly not forthcoming, citing only "increasing cost and complexities." This perceived reluctance to share relevant details angered not only the small group of impacted booksellers but also the majority of vendors who would not even be directly affected by the change.

As reflected in this statement by Britain's Antiquarian Books Association — it wasn't necessarily what AbeBooks did that upset people, it was how they did it.

> "AbeBooks are entitled to do business where they like, as are all other businesses. It is not the decision itself that has led to this unprecedented uprising of dealers across the world, but the high-handed manner in which they dismissed these few rare booksellers, destroying their livelihoods in just a couple of impersonal sentences."[2]

600 booksellers in 26 countries joined the strike of AbeBooks, removing some 2 million items from the marketplace. In response to press inquiries, AbeBooks gave a few more details on its decision: its third-party payment processor in several countries was closing, and therefore, it felt it could no longer support vendors in those locations. Or…could it?

After just a few days, the strike was over. AbeBooks had changed course — the marketplace would remain open to all vendors; it would find a new payment processor.

While the outcome of this case may be surprising, the vendors' reaction to the initial change communication is not. Those who crafted that email — and the rest of us as well — would benefit from understanding that during change, people look for useful and timely information, which adequately answers their questions, and acknowledges the impact of the change.[3]

What is "change communication"?

A basic definition of communication is "the exchange of information or news." While that definition also holds for communication during times of organizational change, a more precise definition of change communication might be:

> *The continuous, multi-directional exchange of relevant information between all impacted parties, in both formal and informal ways.*

As demonstrated by these definitions, *change* communication is communication — but it's nuanced. In this chapter, we'll focus on that nuance.

Why communication during change matters

A variety of research indicates that effective communication during organizational change is linked to important outcomes such as increased trust, job satisfaction, and openness to change as well as decreased anxiety, uncertainty, and stress.[4]

It's important to realize, though, that communication is not a panacea. It won't eliminate all unfortunate outcomes of a change — such as a sense of uncertainty during a restructuring or a decrease in satisfaction during a pay freeze. However, multiple studies have demonstrated that adverse outcomes related to a change tend to stabilize over time amongst those who are provided explanations and opportunities to ask questions. However, negative outcomes tend to grow amongst those who are not provided such opportunities.[5]

The basics of effective change communication

Volumes have been written on the ins and outs of effective communication during change. Here, we'll stick to essential ideas and practices that can help set you up for success.

Anticipating the expected

Change is full of uncertainty for those impacted as well as those leading the change. We can't see around all corners; however, we can anticipate the expected by understanding some of the typical dynamics at play during organizational change.

During times of change, people are generally looking for information that is useful, timely, and which adequately answers their questions.

What questions are they likely to have?

Some will be unique to the impacted individual or group. However, research on change readiness highlights topics that will likely be of interest to all affected stakeholders, including:[6]

- **The Need** — Is the change necessary? How do we know? Are the vision and purpose of the change clear? Is the change aligned with the organization's strategy?
- **Right Solution** — Is the proposed innovation a good fit for the need, culture, and capacity of the organization? What alternatives were considered? How was the final decision made?
- **Change Capability** — Is the organization (and individuals within it) capable of implementing the change? Do the necessary skills and capabilities exist, or can they be learned?
- **Support** — Does the organization (and specific leaders within it) support the change? How do they demonstrate support for the change through words, actions, and resourcing? What is the relative importance of this change?
- **Impact** — How and how much will things change? Will the change create winners and losers? What specific differences will people experience in their roles, responsibilities, pay, or performance expectations?

These readiness factors provide a nice starting point for your change communication. You can develop key messages for each topic and use them consistently throughout the implementation.

For more complex changes or those that are broad in scope, you may need to make adjustments to these messages for specific stakeholder groups. Doing so requires that you identify all stakeholders impacted by the change and understand their fundamental interests or concerns. For more on stakeholder analysis, see the Stakeholders chapter.

Make communication a two-way street

Although stakeholder participation or engagement in change decisions is commonly thought to increase performance or satisfaction, a review of research indicates its practical impact in that regard is likely small at best. Providing opportunities for participation so that people "feel involved" may be necessary to align with an organization's culture, but does not seem to be an effective strategy in terms of change outcomes. A better choice may be to design engagement opportunities to enable the exchange of unique information and perspectives across groups. Such knowledge-sharing can lead to improved decision-making related to the innovation and change process.[7]

To support such knowledge-sharing, your change communication plans should include a variety of opportunities for dialog between the stakeholders involved in the change. The chance to participate can be offered in many forms, from pulse surveys, to focus groups, design sessions, interviews, hotlines, email support, collaboration software or messaging, internal social networks, or simply sharing a cup of coffee. It can also be worthwhile to consider how you can enable people to actively "pull" information about the change when they want it (a form of participation) and not limit access to occasions when you "push" information out to them.

For more discussion on end user participation, please see the End Users chapter.

Multiple methods, trusted messengers, and repetition

One and done is not an advisable communication strategy, even for small-scale changes. You'll need to repeat key messages via a variety of methods — formal, informal, written, verbal, virtual, face-to-face. You'll also want to provide pertinent information throughout the full life-cycle of the change, not just at the beginning. It can be helpful to remember that those more deeply involved in the change effort do a lot more thinking about the change than those who are only hearing about it during special meetings or via emails or video messages. People need time, and multiple chances, to digest information and make sense of it.

Who is doing the communicating may also make a difference. Some research suggests that people look to executives for strategic information, but may anticipate that their managers will deliver more tactical information about the implementation process.[8] While we often look to those with positional authority to deliver change messages, trust should also be a consideration. It is wise to identify leaders who have built trust amongst critical stakeholders to be part of your communication efforts.

Keep in mind that people also look to their networks for information. When identifying members of stakeholder groups to act as change agents, know that opinion leaders may be more effective in the role than employees chosen at random.[9]

Finally, it's essential to remember that actions speak as loud as, (or louder than), words. A mismatch between change messages and leader actions, or a change agent's words and behaviors, can negatively impact trust, commitment, and performance of stakeholders involved in the implementation.[10] Don't assume everyone shares awareness of this point — take steps to support those representing the change to embody their role fully. For more on developing change leadership capabilities, see the Leadership chapter.

Phases and Communication

Plan to communicate throughout the life of the change. While some key messages will serve you well throughout the implementation, you'll also need to craft phase-specific communication. Doing so will help you provide timely and relevant information, rather than overwhelming your audience or leaving them in the dark.

For instance, during the **Decide** phase, you may want to focus on building awareness of the need and vision for the change and share the chosen innovation. This is also an excellent time to highlight what's not changing. Providing information and getting input on plans for roll-out as well as adapting the selected innovation is often the focus of the **Prepare** phase. During **Execution**, emphasize the support that is available to those impacted by the change, have clear channels for feedback and keep everyone updated on progress.

The **Improve** phase requires robust two-way communication to enable you to identify impactful enhancements with input from stakeholders. It's also important for you to demonstrate to people see how their contributions were used to make the innovation and implementation process better, during this phase. During the **Maintain** phase, communicate to build an understanding of the transition from implementation to operationalization— e.g., new contacts, sources of support — as well as highlighting achievements and gathering perspectives on lessons learned.

STARTER STEPS: Communication

Communication is an essential tool to build trust, awareness, and understanding during times of change. Leverage the key ideas below to keep your efforts on track.

1. **Develop principles to guide your communication.** Work with your sponsor and implementation team to identify a few fundamental values that you aim to uphold through your change communication effort. For example, providing timely and accurate information, demonstrating respect, or ensuring people have opportunities to ask questions or provide input.

2. **Identify all impacted stakeholder groups and their key concerns.** Conduct a stakeholder analysis to ensure you deliver information that is relevant from your audiences' perspective and that you don't inadvertently overlook critical groups. For more on stakeholder analysis, see the Stakeholders chapter.

3. **Use a change readiness framework and implementation phases to shape key messages.** While you will likely need to develop communication beyond those suggested through these tools, they provide a checklist of essential topics you should address at a minimum.

4. **Don't wing it.** A simple communication plan that highlights who, what, how, when, and why will help you cover your bases and stay on track. For more on Planning, see the Infrastructure chapter.

EXPERT TIPS

Build capacity for dialog. Not everyone is a born communicator or capable of facilitating a constructive dialog when emotions run high, which they can during times of change. Actively coach those who act as the face of the change to ensure they feel prepared and capable to listen and learn, as well as speak and direct.

Integrate communication across components. Ensure that change messages are incorporated into training and coaching and that formal communications draw on learning from measurement and monitoring efforts.

Use existing infrastructure. Integrate your change communication into the existing communication infrastructure in your organization where possible. Doing so will help people find your information where they already are, instead of requiring them to come to you.

Evaluate your effort. Check-in with audiences formally and informally to ensure that your change messaging is hitting the mark — is it timely, useful, relevant, and respectful?

Notes

1. (2018). AbeBooks closes accounts and withdraws from several markets. Retrieved from https://ilab.org/articles/abebooks-closes-accounts-and-withdraws-several-markets
2. Flood, A. (2018c). Booksellers unite in protest as Amazon's AbeBooks withdraws from several countries. Retrieved from Retrieved from https://www.theguardian.com/books/2018/nov/06/booksellers-protest-amazon-abebooks-withdraw-russia-south-korea
3. Miller, K., & Monge, P. (1985). Social information and employee anxiety about organizational change. *Human Communication Research*, 11(3), 365-386. doi: 10.1111/j.1468-2958.1985.tb00052.x
4. Van Dam, K., Oreg, S., & Schyns, B. (2008). Daily work contexts and resistance to organisational change: The role of leader–member exchange, development climate, and change process characteristics. *Applied Psychology*, 57(2), 313-334. doi: 10.1111/j.1464-0597.2007.00311x
5. See, for example, Schaubroeck, J., May, D. R., & Brown, F. W. (1994). Procedural justice explanations and employee reactions to economic hardship: A field experiment. *Journal of Applied Psychology*, 79(3), 455. doi: 10.1037/0021-9010.79 and Schweiger, D. M., & Denisi, A. S. (1991). Communication with employees following a merger: A longitudinal field experiment. *Academy of Management Journal*, 34(1), 110-135. doi: 10.5465/256304
6. This list was adapted from the readiness framework outlined in Rafferty, A. E., Jimmieson, N. L., & Armenakis, A. A. (2013). Change readiness: A multilevel review. *Journal of Management*, 39(1), 110-135. doi:10.1177/0149206312457417
7. For further discussion on participation and change, see ten Have, S., ten Have, W., Huijsmans, A. B., & Otto, M. (2016). *Reconsidering Change Management: Applying evidence-based insights in change management practice*. Routledge.
8. Hartge, T., Callahan, T., & King, C. (2018). Leaders' Behaviors During Radical Change Processes: Subordinates' Perceptions of How Well Leader Behaviors Communicate Change. *International Journal of Business Communication*, 56(1), 100-121. doi: 10.1177/2329488415605061
9. Lam, S. S. K., & Schaubroeck, J. (2000). A field experiment testing frontline opinion leaders as change agents. *Journal of Applied Psy-*

chology, 85(6), 987. Retrieved from doi.org/10.1037/ 0021-9010.85.6.987

10. See, for example, Hartge, T., Callahan, T., & King, C. (2018). Leaders' Behaviors During Radical Change Processes: Subordinates' Perceptions of How Well Leader Behaviors Communicate Change. *International Journal of Business Communication, 56*(1), 100-121. doi: 10.1177/2329488415605061 or Simons, T., Leroy, H., Collewaert, V., & Masschelein, S. (2015). How Leader Alignment of Words and Deeds Affects Followers: A Meta-analysis of Behavioral Integrity Research. *Journal of Business Ethics, 132*(4), 831-844. doi:10.1007/s10551-014-2332-3

PART V: WHO

In this section, we discuss the people who make implementation happen and how to engage with them to improve your efforts. Specifically, we'll look at the four key roles in any implementation: the implementation team, leadership, end users, and stakeholders.

THE IMPLEMENTATION TEAM

Mandate, skills, and structure

All implementation teams are not created equal

How might the responsiveness of an implementation team influence end users' perceptions of an innovation? That's the question two IT researchers wanted to answer. To do so, they set up an experiment at a telecommunications company that was implementing a new Customer Relationship Management (CRM) system at several of its locations. An implementation team supported the roll-out of the CRM at both locations, which were functionally similar. The team had the same mandate at both sites: to provide a system that met end users' needs and to help them effectively work with that system.

However, at one site, end users accessed the implementation team through a hotline, where they could report issues and ask questions. System issues reported to the hotline were handled using standard procedures. At the other site, implementation team members were often physically present to answer questions and facilitate quick turnaround on bugs and functionality requests, in addition to being available via a hotline. What was the result of the experiment?

The end users who received a high level of responsiveness from the implementation team perceived the team to be significantly more cooperative, had more favorable views of the CRM system, and were more likely to adopt the system than the end users that accessed the team only via a hotline.[1]

Sometimes called change agents, integrators, or coordinators, implementation teams are a central factor in effective implementation. In fact, one review of 25 implementation frameworks found that nearly 70% of them included the development of an implementation team as an essential step.[2]

In this chapter, we review the factors involved in developing a successful implementation team, drawing from research on teams in general, as well as that particular to implementation teams. Specifically, we'll look at three areas:

1. Mandate, which relates to the purpose, boundaries, and accountability of the implementation team.

2. Skills and perspectives, which covers the mix of capabilities and viewpoints necessary to support the implementation.

3. Structure, which focuses on how the team is organized and positioned within the larger organizational context.

To begin, though, we'll take a step back and review why an implementation team is even needed.

Why Is an Implementation Team Necessary?

When I think of implementation teams, I often recall a conversation I had with an executive about the design and implementation of a new process. After we covered fundamental questions about the purpose and desired outcomes of the change, I asked: "So, who on your staff is available to lead the implementation?" The executive responded: "Well…everyone! Everyone will be involved and leading from day one. It will be just how we do things!"

Everyone.

The trick is that for everyone to play a role in "leading" the change, they need direction and support. Even super-committed, high-performing staff need guidance. Even when the change "is part of their job," they need help getting up to speed. Even when the change is well designed and documented, questions and problems may arise that need to be worked through and worked out. Even when you are confident the change will lead to great outcomes, you need to measure and track progress, just to be sure. Someone, not everyone, should be responsible for these types of things.

Initial research indicates that it's often a good bet for that "someone" to be an implementation team.

Some researchers suggest that a team, rather than individual change agents, may offer several advantages. A team may be more able to sustain momentum and motivation, offer diverse skills that can support the complex requirements of change implementation, and have greater credibility with stakeholders.[3]

For all these reasons, establishing a team that is accountable for the implementation seems pretty important. Just creating a team won't make it successful, however. It needs to have a clear purpose, supportive structure, and members with requisite skills and perspectives, among other things.

Mandate

Focused on the successful execution of a particular change

Implementation teams are differentiated from other types of teams by their mandate. Fundamentally, the implementation team is responsible for the successful execution of a particular change — full stop. Individual members of the implementation team may have job responsibilities beyond their work on the team; however, the focus of their activities on the implementation team should relate to a specific and defined change.

Responsible for the design and management of the implementation

Some may conceptualize implementation teams as solely for the management of change execution. However, in practice, all implementation teams are involved to some degree in both the design of the innovation being implemented and the management of efforts to embed the innovation in the organization. For example, teams created only after a decision has been made on what to implement will still be involved in design tasks when they refine and improve the innovation based on initial implementation results.

Not a governance body or steering committee

The implementation team should not be confused with a governance body, steering committee, or management team. While the team will likely have some decision-making authority, it often relies on others, such as the executive sponsor or governance body, for strategic decisions. What's more, this is not a team that does the majority of its work around a conference room table. It's a team that is on its feet, working shoulder to shoulder with leaders and end users. It is a roll up your sleeves and dig in the dirt group of people.

Not a group of adopters or end users

The implementation team is also distinct from end users. The best implementation teams often include representatives of the end user community; however, an implementation team is not simply an organized group of adopters. Rather, it brings to bear specific skills and perspectives to support the implementation, as outlined in the next section.

Skills and Perspectives

To fulfill its mandate, the implementation team must include members with a variety of capabilities as well as insights. For this reason, when creating the implementation team, it's important to consider requirements for hard skills, as well as diverse organizational perspectives.

Skills

Specific skills often represented on an implementation team include:

Project management: Project management skills support effective planning, budgeting, scheduling, execution management, and liaising with the governance body and key stakeholders.

Innovation-specific expertise: Someone with a high degree of competence related to the innovation being implemented (e.g., software, process, or practice) is necessary to inform design, planning, training, and coaching. Such skill is often provided by external consultants or vendors, but may also be sourced internally. Including folks who have experience and knowledge of good practice in implementation is also a good idea!

Training and coaching: Training is more than developing and reviewing PowerPoint presentations with a group of end users. For this reason, each team should include members skilled in the design and delivery of training and ongoing technical assistance.

Measurement and analysis: Measurement skills are critical to enable the team to monitor the implementation, gather feedback, assess outcomes, and identify necessary improvements.

Communication and engagement: The team should include individuals with the ability to tell the story of the implementation in ways that are meaningful to various audiences. For this reason, those with talents in engagement and listening are also good to include on the team's roster.

Teamwork and collaboration: It's also wise to consider individuals' teamwork and collaboration abilities, to avoid assembling a group of experts who act independently, rather than as an interdependent team.

(For more about these skill areas, see Part IV.)

Perspectives

Change is often viewed differently at different levels of the organization. Executives and front-line staff will have unique concerns and hopes for the innovation being implemented. They may also anticipate and be able to help mitigate distinct types of challenges.

For this reason, several researchers have highlighted the importance of diverse organizational representation on the implementation team.[4] They suggest drawing team members from all levels of the organizational hierarchy, as well as all pertinent functional areas. Doing so ensures that a comprehensive set of perspectives inform design, planning, and execution. It may also ensure the team has the required power and influence necessary to carry out its mandate.

Can team members change over time?

The literature on teams indicates that stability of members is often necessary to attain high levels of team performance.[5] The argument goes, if people are constantly cycling on and off of the team, it can be hard to develop a rhythm or even to know who's a team member. This makes sense.

However, given that implementation efforts can be long-term affairs — lasting anywhere from one to three years or more — the ideal of team member stability may be hard to attain. Therefore, some suggest that we should instead focus on functional or role stability, rather than the consistency of particular individuals.[6] For example, you can aim to have project management and front-line staff functions represented, rather than making sure that Nigel from the PMO and Sondra from customer service are always on the team.

Structure

So, you've got a clear mandate. You've selected team members with a comprehensive set of skills and perspectives. How do you structure the team to be both inclusive and manageable?

No single structure works well for all implementations. However, there are general considerations that I have found to be useful when structuring implementation teams, including:

- Ensure the structure clarifies accountabilities and distinguishes between the implementation team, governance body, end users, and other stakeholders.
- Segment the implementation team into sub-teams or auxiliary teams to ensure it remains both inclusive and manageable. When teams grow larger than about five members, they often benefit from additional structure.
- Assign members to act as formal liaisons to particular end user groups or stakeholders.

Figure 10 provides an example of a general implementation team structure that reflects these considerations.

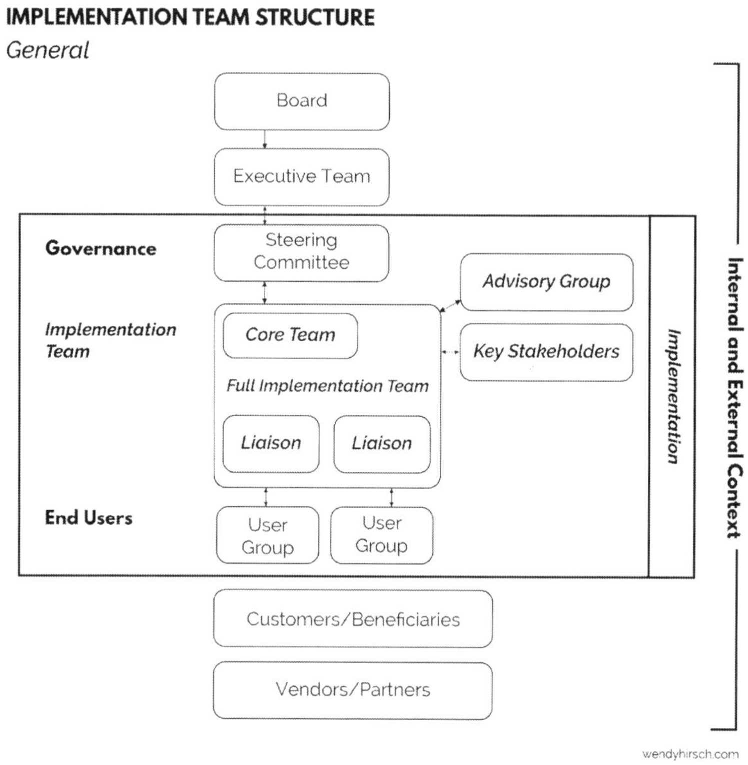

IMPLEMENTATION TEAM STRUCTURE
General

```
                        Board
                          │
                    Executive Team
                          │
Governance          Steering
                    Committee
                                        Advisory Group
Implementation       Core Team
Team                                    Key Stakeholders
                 Full Implementation Team

                  Liaison    Liaison

End Users          User       User
                   Group      Group

                Customers/Beneficiaries

                   Vendors/Partners
```

(Internal and External Context; Implementation)

Figure 10 — General Team Structure

Clarify accountabilities and linkages with the larger context

The structure of the team should reflect its mandate. To that end, the boundaries and linkages between the implementation team, the governance body, and stakeholders should be clear. This can help to reflect the accountability and responsibilities of the implementation team (versus others) and encourage team members to remain aware of the larger context in which they are working.

Consider segmenting the team

Particularly on larger or longer-term efforts, it can be useful to create sub-teams or auxiliary teams. For instance, developing a core team of two to three individuals charged with project management and stakeholder engagement tasks can help streamline these efforts, and keep the rest of the team focused on other aspects of the implementation.

If you find yourself in a situation where a desire to be inclusive is likely to cause the implementation team to be so large it's unmanageable, consider creating an advisory group. Doing so allows you to keep your implementation team small, while also benefiting from the unique experience of persons who might not have the time or interest in full-time membership on the team. This tactic also helps you to avoid having an implementation team with members who serve in name only, rarely doing any work or even attending meetings.

If you do create such an advisory group, be sure its mandate is distinguished from that of the implementation team and governance body, and communicated upfront to all potential members. Generally speaking, you'd ask this body to review and respond to specific questions at defined points during the planning or execution of the effort.

Membership in the advisory group ordinarily requires less time and work than full implementation team membership. However, advisory group members are usually more informed and involved in the implementation than general stakeholders. As a result, the implementation team often will give more weight to input from the advisory group than input received through other forms of engagement (e.g., surveys, focus groups, town hall meetings).

Establish liaisons or key contacts

Consider assigning members of the implementation team to act as liaisons or key contacts with particular end user groups. Such liaisons can help end users adjust the innovation to meet their unique needs, challenges, and opportunities, while also ensuring the integrity of the innovation. Key contacts can also put a personal face on the implementation and provide reassurance to adopters and end users. Knowing there is a person to go to with questions or concerns, rather than addressing them to a large group or anonymous email address, can make a difference.

Implementation Teams in Action

It can be difficult to understand structural considerations in the abstract. So, let's look at how the generic structure discussed in the previous section comes to life in various real-world situations. Specifically, we'll look at teams involved in the implementation of an Enterprise Resource Planning (ERP) system, a process improvement effort, and a system-wide strategy.

Although the context, scale, and content of each case are different, you'll notice how the key structural elements of the implementation teams are largely the same. First, the implementation team, governance body, and end user groups are differentiated from one another. Second, the membership on the implementation team is evident; it is sometimes also segmented into sub-teams and augmented by additional groups. Finally, there are defined liaisons tasked with supporting key end user groups.

ERP implementation at a car manufacturer

To run the implementation of an ERP, a luxury car manufacturer created an implementation team, headed by its IT department. The implementation team was led by a core team comprised of managers from IT as well as technical specialists from the ERP vendor. Because the IT department was itself outsourced and managed by contractors, the team also included managers from other business units at the company who had knowledge of internal processes, systems, and organizational culture. Finally, the implementation team included planning teams from each operational unit, who managed training and process changes within their unit.[7]

IMPLEMENTATION TEAM STRUCTURE
Enterprise Resource Planning (ERP)

- Governance: Management Team → IT Leadership
- Implementation Team:
  - Core Team: IT Manager, ERP Specialist
  - Implementation Team: IT Managers, ERP Specialist, Business Unit Managers
  - Planning Team, Planning Team
- End Users: Business Unit, Business Unit

wendyhirsch.com

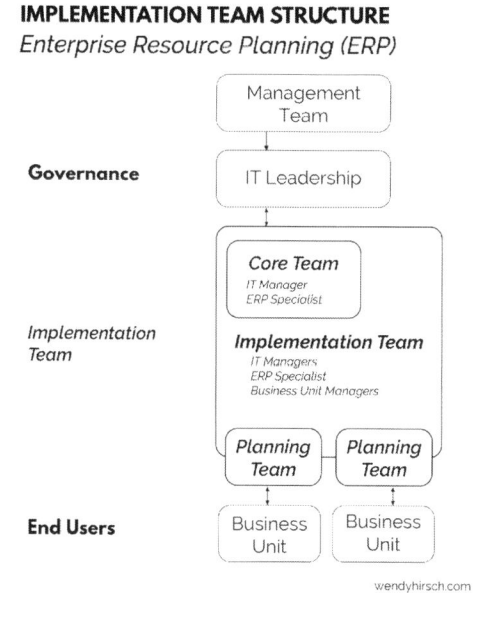

Figure 11 — ERP Structure

Process improvement in a healthcare organization

A community healthcare organization in Britain created an implementation team to oversee a business process improvement program, which they executed as part of their contract with the National Health Service (NHS). The NHS provided goals and targets for the effort; however, the method of implementation was left largely to the organization.

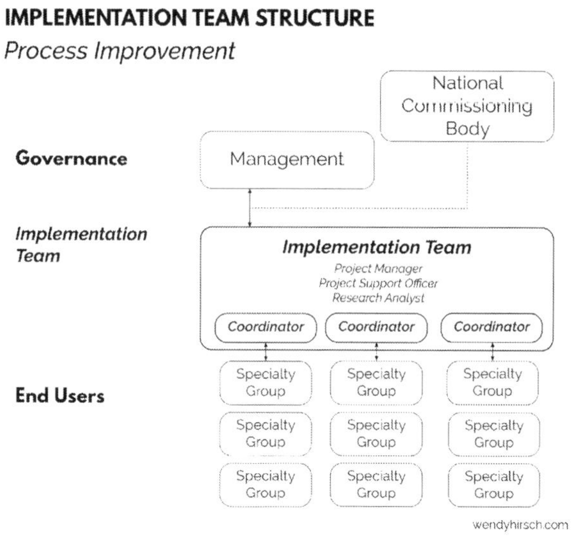

IMPLEMENTATION TEAM STRUCTURE
Process Improvement

Figure 12 – Process Improvement Structure

The implementation team consisted of a project manager, a project support officer, and a research analyst, as well as three nurse coordinators. Two nurses were employees, and one was hired as a contractor. These coordinators interfaced with each of 38 specialty groups involved as end users in the implementation. The coordinators mainly worked with the managers of these specialty groups, but sometimes worked directly with staff using the innovation.[8]

System-wide strategy implementation

South Africa recently put in place a national strategy to revamp how community healthcare workers support primary healthcare throughout the country. The strategy included broad changes such as new goals, ways of engaging with community members, as well as updated roles and relationships between different actors in the primary healthcare system. This example reflects the implementation team in one province.

IMPLEMENTATION TEAM STRUCTURE
System-wide Strategy

```
                    ┌─────────────┐
                    │  National   │
                    │ Department  │
                    │  of Health  │
                    └──────┬──────┘
Governance              ┌──┴──────────┐
                        │  Provincial │
                        │ Management  │
                        └──────┬──────┘
Implementation    ┌────────────┴──────────┐       ┌──────────┐
Team              │  Implementation Team  │──────│  Health   │
                  │                       │       │  Systems  │
                  │ Provincial Directors  │       │   Trust   │
                  │ Representative HST    │       └──────────┘
                  │ Provincial Rep.       │       ┌──────────┐
                  │ Coordinator           │──────│ District  │
                  └───────────────────────┘       │Management│
                                                  │  Teams   │
                                                  └──────────┘
                     District    District
                    Coordinator Coordinator  ○ ○ ○
                     Sub-Dist.   Sub-Dist.
                    Coordinator Coordinator  ○ ○ ○
                    Managers/   Managers/
                    Team Leads  Team Leads   ○ ○ ○
End Users            Faculty     Faculty     ○ ○ ○
                    Community   Community    ○ ○ ○
```

wendyhirsch.com

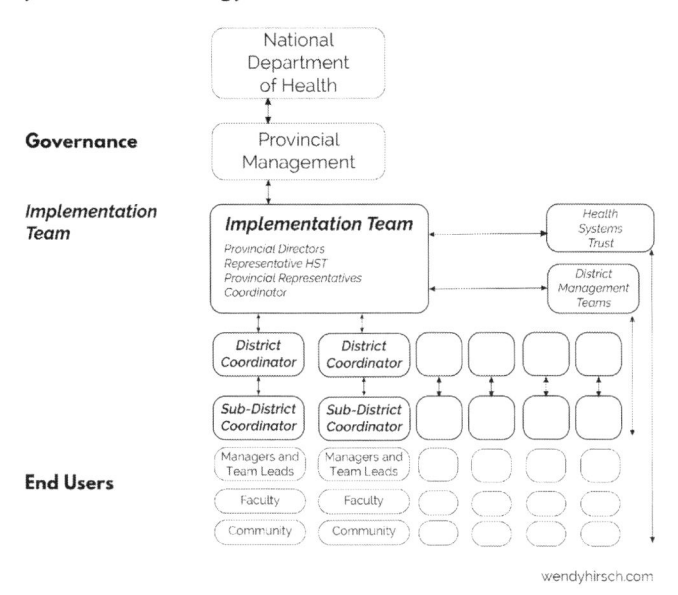

Figure 13 — System-wide Strategy Structure

The implementation team oversaw implementation plans, communication, progress monitoring, and troubleshooting. The team included directors from each district in the province, a representative from the Health Systems Trust, and delegates from various district-level entities (hospitals, finance, monitoring and evaluation, HR, etc.). The group also included a full-time coordinator who worked across the province, as well as coordinators at the district and sub-district levels who served as a link between the implementation team and managers and team leaders at the district level.

In addition to the implementation team, representatives from the Health Systems Trust provided technical assistance to all levels of the effort. District management teams remained involved by consistently carving out time for discussion of the implementation during their meetings.[9]

As these cases demonstrate, although the nature of the implementations they led was quite different, the teams were structured in similar ways. When putting these ideas into practice on your next implementation, aim to start with the simplest structure possible. Then add on as necessary to clarify differences between roles, support the efficient functioning of the team, and provide explicit support to end users.

Developing a High-Performing Implementation Team

Clarifying the team's mandate, as well as staffing and structuring it appropriately, will put your team in a great position to begin its work. Beyond that, implementation teams benefit from good practices that support high-performing teams in general, such as:[10]

Support better cooperation on the team by encouraging team members to discuss past experiences. This can familiarize team members with the abilities of their colleagues and help to build trust. In addition, structure work to provide the opportunity for early wins to build the team's confidence in their collective abilities.

Improve coordination on your team by establishing clear routines and roles. Routines and roles help the team save time and energy — everyone already knows what to do and who is going to do it. However, when routines or roles are too strict, they can inhibit the team from adapting to changing circumstances or addressing flagging performance. It's a good idea to provide some flexibility to allow the team to adjust. A practice of regular team debriefs to identify required changes is also useful.

Promote effective communication by using a consistent framework to structure conversations (e.g., purpose, discussion, conclusions, and next steps). It can also be useful to set expectations for members to confirm receipt of emails, memos, or other forms of messaging. Co-located teams may benefit from sharing their specialized skills and experiences. To help virtual teams develop a shared social context, (associated with cohesion and trust), create opportunities for team members to meet in person on occasion and use video-conferencing in addition to email or messaging apps.

Enhance team learning by cultivating a team culture where it feels safe to ask questions, share ideas, and take risks. Leaders can help set the tone by being open to questions and encouraging team members to learn from mistakes.

(For more techniques that can help you to develop a high-performing team, I invite you to explore my blog posts on team leadership at wendyhirsch.com.)

Phases and the Implementation Team

During the **Decide** phase, you'll work with leadership to secure the people resources necessary to support the implementation. These may include monetary resources for contracting with external specialists, as well as a commitment to reassign staff to the effort. During the **Prepare** phase, you'll select team members, structure the team, and develop team processes and norms. During this phase, team members will be engaged in planning as well as preparing training, coaching, and measurement and monitoring efforts.

During the **Execute** phase, the team will essentially work the plan — train, coach, collect and analyze data, engage with stakeholders, and troubleshoot issues. During the **Improve** phase, the team will identify improvements that should be made to the innovation or approach for future execution cycles. (Depending on the governance structure for the effort, the team may decide which improvements to undertake or need to seek approval from leadership.) Once improvements are identified, the team will need to act on them, e.g., updating the innovation and related documentation and team processes.

Finally, before their departure from the team, in anticipation or support of the **Maintain** phase, team members should be involved in identifying lessons, updating and archiving materials, and transitioning their primary areas of responsibility to new owners.

STARTER STEPS: Implementation Team

Although the requirements for each implementation team will be unique, there are common elements you should keep in mind as you develop your team, which include:

1. **Clarify the implementation team's mandate.** Doing so often involves answering questions such as: What are the team's specific accountabilities? How are these different from that of other groups? Where does the team have autonomy? What are the limits to its autonomy? What is the anticipated lifespan of the team?

2. **Identify required skills and perspectives.** Beyond standard skills often represented on implementation teams, such a project management, identify unique needs you may have. What technical skills are required to ensure the effective design of the innovation and to support training? Which interest groups should be represented on the team?

3. **Develop a structure.** Start with a basic structure that supports the team's mandate and distinguishes it from other groups. Augment it as necessary with sub-teams or auxiliary groups that have clear, complementary remits.

EXPERT TIPS

Create a formal team. Resist the temptation to think you can lead the effort alone, or by calling on others in an ad hoc way.

Get explicit commitment from individuals and their managers when selecting implementation team members. Provide an estimate of the time required from team members and ensure it is realistic. Avoid having members who serve in name only.

Focus on the stability of functions and roles, not individuals. Rather than trying to retain specific individuals on the team throughout the lifespan of the implementation, which may not be possible, aim to ensure key roles and functions are consistently filled.

Get knowledgeable about good team practice. Brush up on your team development and management skills to help you provide the guidance, structure, and support your team needs to succeed.

Notes

1. This case was adapted from Gefen, D. & Ridings, C. (2002). Implementation team responsiveness and user evaluation of customer relationship management: A quasi-experimental design study of social exchange theory. *Journal of Management Information Systems, 19*(1), 47-69. doi: 10.1080/07421222.2002.11045717
2. See Meyers, D. C., Durlak, J. A., & Wandersman, A. (2012). The quality implementation framework: A synthesis of critical steps in the implementation process. *American Journal of Community Psychology, 50*(3-4), 462-480. doi:10.1007/s10464-012-9522-x
3. See, for example, Hackman, J. R., & Edmondson, A. C. (2008). Groups as agents of change. In T. Cummings (Ed.), *Handbook of organization development* (pp. 167-186). Thousand Oaks, CA: Sage.
4. See, for example, Higgins, M. C., Weiner, J., & Young, L. (2012). Implementation teams: A new lever for organizational change. *Journal of Organizational Behavior, 33*(3), 366-388. doi:10.1002/job.1773, and Hackman, J. R., & Edmondson, A. C. (2008). Groups as agents of change. In T. Cummings (Ed.), *Handbook of organization development* (pp. 167-186). Thousand Oaks, CA: Sage.
5. See, for example, Hackman, J. R., and Wageman, R. "When and how team leaders matter." *Research in Organizational Behavior, 26*, 37-74. doi:10.1016/S0191-3085(04)26002-6
6. See Higgins, M. C., Weiner, J., & Young, L. (2012). Implementation teams: A new lever for organizational change. *Journal of Organizational Behavior, 33*(3), 366-388. doi:10.1002/job.1773
7. This example was adapted from Yusuf, Y., Gunasekaran, A., & Abthorpe, M. S. (2004). Enterprise information systems project implementation: A case study of ERP in Rolls-Royce. *International Journal of Production Economics, 87*(3), 251-266. https://doi.org/10.1016/j.ijpe.2003.10.004
8. This example was adapted from Bradley, D. K. F., & Griffin, M. (2016). The Well Organised Working Environment: A mixed methods study. *International Journal of Nursing Studies, 55*, 26-38. Retrieved from http://repository.essex.ac.uk/id/eprint/15543
9. This example was adapted from Schneider, H., English, R., Tabana, H., Padayachee, T., & Orgill, M. (2014). Whole-system change: Case study of factors facilitating early implementation of a primary health care reform in a South African province. *BMC Health Services Research, 14*(1). 609. doi: 10.1186/s12913-014-0609-y

10. For a helpful overview, see Salas, E., Shuffler, M. L., Thayer, A. L., Bedwell, W. L., & Lazzara, E. H. (2015). Understanding and improving teamwork in organizations: A scientifically based practical guide. *Human Resource Management, 54*(4), 599-622. doi: 10.1002/hrm.21628

LEADERSHIP

The sponsor, governance body, and middle management

Problems mount as leaders fail to act

In October 2013, as part of the implementation of its landmark healthcare bill, the United States government launched the healthcare.gov website. The site was supposed to function as an online store where consumers could purchase health insurance plans made available through the law. It was a huge deal! Except — the site crashed within two hours of launch. On the first day, only six people were able to sign up, although at least 40,000 tried. It was a failure of epic proportions.

Although inadequate project management, poor contracting practices, and cultural issues all contributed to the disastrous launch, the top reason for the failure was a fundamental lack of leadership. As noted in one study, "…the absence of clear leadership…caused delays in decision-making, lack of clarity in project tasks, and the inability…to recognize the magnitude of problems as the project deteriorated."

Fortunately, within months, the site was mostly fixed and able to manage an increasing volume of visitors. The turnaround was attributed to significant changes in the way the effort was led, including a "ruthless" focus on prioritization and the establishment of a badgeless culture, where both staff and contractors worked together as a single team. Also, a top administrator took the role of "Federal Marketplace Leader," attending detailed briefings and making timely decisions to correct management issues. This role eventually became a new CEO position, a first for the agency overseeing the marketplace.[1]

Leaders in implementation come from all levels and functions in the organization. Leadership, in its broadest sense, is needed from front-line staff, supervisors, members of the implementation team, interested stakeholders, as well as senior management. The idea that a single, heroic leader solely guides the organization through change does not generally play out in reality.

At the same time, successful implementations require an explicit source of direction and support. Even deeply participatory implementations usually have a person or defined group responsible for clarifying the vision, making tough decisions, and demonstrating the organization's commitment to the effort. It's this more focused type of leadership that we'll discuss in this chapter.

Such leadership is usually provided via several different roles. One is the sponsor, also known as the change champion. The second is the governance body, sometimes called the steering committee or governance council. The last is an intermediary role, usually played by middle managers or supervisors.

In my experience, many people who take on these change leadership positions don't have a good understanding of what it takes to execute them well. Even those who are committed and willing may not understand the nuances of leading during times of change. In such cases, staff involved in the implementation, or external consultants, may need to provide these leaders with coaching or other development opportunities. As such, this chapter is a worthwhile read for everyone involved in the effort, not just those who anticipate holding formal leadership positions in an implementation.

The Sponsor

Is the sponsor always an executive?

The primary responsibilities of the sponsor are to clarify and communicate the vision for the implementation, ensure required resourcing and infrastructure is available to support the effort, and remove obstacles that the implementation team cannot overcome on its own. The person(s) playing the sponsor role needs to have the authority necessary to carry out such actions.

Although an executive often plays the sponsor role, the role is not always filled from the highest levels of the organizational hierarchy. For example, if the implementation impacts the entire organization, such as a strategy implementation or restructuring, the executive sponsor may be the CEO, or a person in a position directly reporting to her. If the implementation focuses on practices in a single division, or team, perhaps the Director in that division, or the team manager, would be the sponsor. The key is for this person to have the authority and influence required to be effective in the role.

Often, a single person fills the sponsor role. Although multiple people can share the position, it is a complicated structure that makes significant demands on all players to be successful. Shared sponsorship requires strong alignment, which takes time and energy to develop.

To avoid being a source of confusion, the co-sponsors need to align their vision for the implementation and clarify some basic decision-making conventions. (For example, do all co-sponsors need to agree on all decisions? Will co-sponsors share accountability for all aspects of the change or assign specific responsibilities to individual co-sponsors?) Given the degree of effort required for successful co-sponsorship, I recommend adopting it only when the benefits are explicitly articulated and found to outweigh the costs.

What type of leader is required?

When you delve into writing on leadership and organizational change, you'll find a debate about two types of leadership. One being straight-line, command and control direction, sometimes referred to as management or transactional leadership. The other is inspirational, visionary, or motivational guidance, which is sometimes referred to as adaptive, charismatic, or transformational leadership.

Rather than there being one superior type of leader during change, research indicates the complexities of implementation often require the sponsor to exhibit both types of leadership. Sometimes, people just want to be told what to do and their request is reasonable. Decisions need to be made and directions chosen. On the other hand, implementation often involves uncertainty or requires stakeholders to adjust ingrained behaviors and ways of thinking. In such cases, it may not be possible to tell someone "exactly" what they need to do. Instead, such changes demand leadership that builds the confidence of staff members and motivates them to be part of creating the solution, rather than being given a solution.

The right mix of leadership styles for any given effort requires a careful assessment of the nature and context of the implementation. In general, management, or transactional leadership, may be a better match for more certain or stable situations, which don't demand significant shifts in behavior or processes. Adaptive or transformational leadership may be better suited when the innovation being implemented requires action under conditions of considerable uncertainty.[2]

What does the sponsor do?

Over the last 20 years, I have worked with many sponsors. Based on this firsthand experience, as well as published research on the topic, I have identified a few things that most successful sponsors do.[3]

Clarify the need

Sponsors must ensure that the organization invests adequate time and energy in understanding and specifically defining the "problem to be solved." I have worked with several sponsors who talked about having a burning platform. This scenario is one in which the problem is clear. The organization and those in it have no choice but to make a move — jump or you will be burned! A burning platform is undoubtedly compelling. However, change and strategy implementations aren't always undertaken during times of crisis — and it's not necessarily wise to create a crisis when one doesn't exist. Rather, leaders may be required to anticipate and build a case for change when the need is not already obvious to everyone. Using a mix of motivational and rationale messaging may be useful in such situations.[4]

Specify the vision and direction

The sponsor must articulate a vision for the future the change will create. Although the sponsor may have her ideas about the direction of the effort, this vision is often drafted in consultation with others. Further, the sponsor, again often working with others, must ensure that the innovation selected for the implementation is the right one to achieve this vision in the current organizational environment.[5] (Careful readers have likely noted that the ability of the sponsor to do this is linked to an effective process to define desired outcomes and assess the fit of potential innovations to the organization's needs and capabilities, as discussed in Part IV.)

Champion the effort

A champion can be defined as a fierce advocate, a defender, and a supporter. Sponsors are required to be all of these. Although the specific actions the sponsor will take to champion the effort will differ, they often include things such as:

- Building broad support for the change among key stakeholders
- Ensuring the effort is adequately resourced and structured
- Aligning systems and processes to facilitate the change
- Removing obstacles and challenges

Communicate through words and actions

Great sponsors understand that they need to communicate far more than they may want to. If a sponsor isn't desperately tired of talking about the change, she hasn't talked about it nearly enough.

Further, a successful communications effort will not be limited to the sponsor's preferred methods. If a sponsor likes to write, she may send emails. However, the implementation team member who oversees communications may need to create opportunities using other channels as well, such as presentations at all staff meetings or video messages.

An effective sponsor also communicates beyond words, through actions. She models the change she is asking others to make. She demonstrates her commitment to the change, which, particularly during challenging times, can require a willingness to take on a degree of professional risk.

A sponsor can also show support by using her authority and influence to ensure the implementation receives the appropriate degree of attention in the organization. For instance, she might use her influence to secure coverage of the implementation in an internal newsletter or a place on the agenda of staff meetings.

Ensure the proper infrastructure is in place and functioning

Making sure the infrastructure exists to support the implementation may be the aspect of the sponsor role most aligned with the transactional leadership style. To do so, the sponsor must:

- **Establish goals** for the effort and verify that monitoring and measurement plans are in place. The sponsor must be confident that measurement efforts will enable her to answer the question, "Did we succeed?"
- **Confirm that an implementation team and governance structure are in place** and adequately staffed and resourced.
- **Identify and rectify any misalignment** between the change and existing structures in the organization.
- **Engage in the implementation throughout its lifespan** to understand progress to date, provide feedback and encouragement, and offer input on necessary improvements.

Keep in mind, the role of the sponsor is not to micromanage or duplicate the efforts of the implementation lead or team. Preferably, the sponsor and implementation lead or project manager will work together to clarify their respective roles and responsibilities.

The project manager often initiates such conversations with the sponsor at the outset of the effort; however, if she doesn't, the sponsor should. Through these discussions, the sponsor and implementation lead will clarify preferred styles and establish expectations for the amount of time they each will invest in the implementation. Further, they will share what they most need from one another and come to a general agreement on how they will work together.

THE ROLE OF THE SPONSOR
Actions and Attitudes

ACTIONS: *What the Sponsor Does*

- Clarify the need and direction
- Champion the effort
- Communicate! Use words and actions
- Ensure infrastructure is in place

ATTITUDES: *How the Sponsor Does It*

- Be fair and considerate
- Exhibit confidence and commitment
- Welcome questions and encourage ideas

wendyhirsch.com

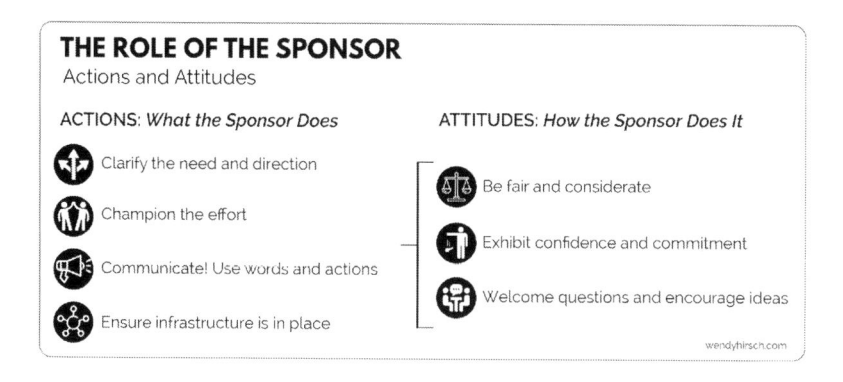

Figure 14 — Role of the Sponsor

How does the sponsor do it?

In addition to specific actions or activities, there are also qualitative aspects of effective sponsorship. This isn't all about personality. I've worked with successful sponsors who have been outgoing and others who are more reserved. It's about the attitudes and behaviors that enable a sponsor to be successful.

Be fair and show you care

The nature of implementation involves asking people to make sacrifices of some kind for the benefit of the organization. Staff members are asked to do things for the greater good. A sponsor can demonstrate fairness and build trust by explaining why people are being asked to change, and sharing not only the outcomes of decisions but also details about how decisions were made. Further, a variety of research indicates that describing how a change will impact people, and acknowledging when a change creates difficult realities, can also be helpful.[6]

Additionally, the sponsor has a significant role to play in regulating the pace and intensity of the implementation. "Faster, harder, and higher" is not always the only and best option. Ronald Heifetz, of Harvard, offers a helpful way to think about this. In his work on adaptive leadership, he writes that leaders must become skilled at creating a "holding environment" that they manage like a pressure cooker — "turning up the heat while allowing some steam to escape."[7]

Not enough heat and nothing will happen, too much heat and you risk an explosion. For example, I worked with a sponsor who kept "the heat turned up" by holding teams accountable for the original goals of the implementation, while "releasing some steam" by adjusting deadlines when they proved to be the source of undue stress.

Exhibit confidence and commitment

A sponsor's confidence can be contagious. Such determination is not derived from omniscience, however. For successful sponsors, it is often grounded in an ability to remain calm and reliable despite uncertainty and ambiguity.

People throughout the organization will always look for signs of waning commitment on the part of the sponsor. Most everyone has had at least one encounter with an organizational change announced with much fanfare, but which produced little. Such experiences are not soon forgotten. Therefore, sponsors should anticipate that at least some impacted staff will take a "wait and see" approach and resist putting too much effort into the implementation. Based on their experience, this tact may be entirely reasonable.

However, if an implementation is to achieve its performance goals, people can't remain on the sidelines for too long. They will if the sponsor appears to be doing so. For this reason, in her words and actions, the effective sponsor telegraphs her commitment to the effort and the support she expects from others, including organizational leadership.

Encourage ideas and welcome questions

As mentioned previously, a successful sponsor is aware of the limits of her knowledge. She does not believe she can or should have all the answers. For this reason, sponsors often facilitate a participative approach to change implementation.

To do so, the sponsor signals openness to questions, as well as new ideas. She understands that successful implementation will likely require input and ingenuity from all levels of the organization. This applies in particular when adoption of the innovation requires significant adjustments in long-held behaviors, norms of operation, and organizational priorities.

At the same time, participatory efforts need to be grounded in cornerstone ideas. Everything cannot be open to debate all the time. Some aspects of the effort must be decided and taken as givens for the process to move forward. The sponsor's leadership can be invaluable in this respect. She can keep her eye trained on the big picture, holding fast to what is known and decided, and asking for input on what is not. An experienced sponsor will also not hesitate too long before making tough calls on areas of debate to keep the effort moving forward.

The Governance Body

The governance body is another source of leadership for the implementation. It is sometimes referred to as the steering committee or governance council. Because the governance body often represents the strategic interests of the organization, it tends to weigh in on foundational aspects of the implementation, such as its purpose, desired outcomes, and budget.

Governance comes in different shapes and sizes

The governance body for the implementation may be a temporary entity created specifically for the effort. In such cases, it is often chaired by the sponsor and will usually have a formal linkage to the broader governance structure of the organization — perhaps reporting to an executive team, the board, or CEO. However, the governance body for the effort may also be a pre-existing group, such as a management team. Governance of the implementation will become part of its remit. In such cases, the sponsor is often a part of the governance body, but may not chair it.

Be explicit and transparent about decision authority

In my experience, many organizations have pretty muddled governance structures. That is hard to fix. However, you can aim to be open about the governance for your implementation. Such clarity can help to avoid the confusion, rework, or paralysis that arises when people are unsure who decides what. Developing a governance framework is a helpful way to outline what types of decisions are made by whom. For more on how to do that, see the Infrastructure chapter.

Usually, the governance body will make strategic decisions on topics such as:

Purpose and desired outcomes: The governance body can make sure the aims of the implementation are aligned with the broader goals of the organization and ensure the objectives are appropriately ambitious.

Resourcing: The governance body may approve the budget for the implementation as well as set expectations for the number of people who will be assigned to the effort. It may also play a role in identifying who will be responsible for the ongoing maintenance of the innovation when the implementation is complete.

Innovation or implementation approach: If the innovation or the implementation approach will significantly impact the people or productivity of the organization, the governance body may get involved with these choices. Otherwise, it may delegate these tasks to the implementation team or sponsor.

Schedule: If the governance body's remit is broader than the implementation, it may play a role in pacing or phasing a multitude of strategic initiatives. As such, the governance body may need to approve the proposed schedule for the implementation, weighing in on start and end dates, or the timing of execution activities that may most impact productivity.

Performance: The governance body often reviews and discusses performance at specific points during the implementation's lifespan. During such reviews, the group may prioritize areas in need of improvement or even decide to discontinue an effort that fails to make sufficient progress.

Over the course of the implementation, the governance body may shift the focus of its decision-making. For instance, if the implementation is progressing well after the first execution cycle, the group may refer more decisions to the sponsor or implementation team. Therefore, it's a good idea to revisit the governance framework at defined points to update accountabilities. Often it can be helpful to do this during the Improve phase.

Support good decision-making with good processes

In addition to knowing what types of decisions the group will make, procedures need to be in place to support the governance body to make such decisions effectively. This includes things such as a set schedule of meetings, clear expectations for the format in which information will be provided to the group, and norms for decision-making (e.g., is a formal voting process used and what happens in the event of an impasse?)

Such procedures may already exist. If they do not, the sponsor can work with the project manager or implementation lead to create them. If the governance body for the implementation is a pre-existing group, you may have less influence on these processes. However, those representing the implementation can ensure that any information they provide to the governance body is pertinent, sufficient to support quality decisions, and timely.

Middle Managers

In many implementations, there is an intermediary leadership role — between end users and the sponsor and governance body. This role is often played by middle managers. This middle tier of management is loosely defined in organizational literature; it can represent those below top-level management but still managers of managers, or first-level supervisors directly managing staff. For our purposes, precisely defining the bounds of this group is not essential.

More important is acknowledging the leadership role middle managers play during change and understanding the demands of this unique position. These leaders are called on to support executives in directing the change, as well as to help staff in adapting to it. To do so effectively requires middle managers to undertake some of the same types of tasks as top-level leaders — communication, mobilization, and evaluation — but with a different emphasis.[8]

Translation

Middle managers are translators during times of change. They often need to adapt messages provided by the core implementation team or sponsor to make them more relevant for those they manage. Additionally, developing detailed plans to support the local-level implementation of the change is frequently part of the middle manager role.

To successfully carry out these facilitative tasks, middle managers need to first make sense of the change for themselves. To understand what it is and how it will impact them personally, as well as the effect it will have on their teams. Sponsors can support middle managers in their translation role by clearly outlining the need, vision, and priorities related to the change. Also helpful is providing time for "sense-making" among middle managers and opportunities for them to interact with those in top-level leadership roles to ask questions and gain clarification.

Getting creative

Leaders at this intermediary level are often required to adjust current operations or secure additional resources to enable the implementation at the local level. For instance, they may provide staff with tools or materials needed to adopt the change, develop local-level monitoring efforts, or manage schedules to allow staff to maintain ongoing operations while also participating in the implementation. The implementation team, sponsor, and other executives can assist middle managers by providing additional resources to support change implementation, developing widely relevant tools or other supports, or adjusting performance expectations during the most demanding stages of the implementation.

A balancing act

Middle managers must also balance a variety of priorities during change implementation. Such balancing can involve demonstrating commitment to the change while also attending to the concerns and emotional needs of staff. Some research indicates middle managers are more effective when they actively do both — not one or the other.[9]

Given their direct relationships with individuals across the organizational hierarchy, middle managers are well positioned to address both the emotional and task-related aspects of change.

However, it is a demanding position and one that may require those who play it to develop new skills. Middle managers can support one another to meet the challenges of the role by creating or leveraging existing peer networks. Centralized assistance can also be provided by the core implementation team through coaching or training to help middle managers develop in their change leadership role.

Phases and Leadership

An active and engaged sponsor and governance body are assets in all phases of an implementation. However, particularly at the start of the effort, during the **Decide** phase, the sponsor and governance body both play a critical role in ensuring the foundational elements of the implementation are established, e.g., the need, vision, and desired outcomes. The outset of the effort is also a crucial time for trust building. Early on, the sponsor should explain what the change is and why it is necessary. In addition, she should signal if impacted staff and others will be engaged in shaping, not just enacting, the innovation that is being implemented.

Further, during the **Prepare** phase, the sponsor, and potentially the governance body, will be well positioned to influence the planned pace and schedule for the effort. During this phase, middle managers may also provide input into the development of the innovation and plans for implementation.

Throughout the **Execute** phase, the sponsor and governance body should actively monitor progress. The sponsor, in particular, will help the implementation team overcome obstacles, and communicate and engage with staff. Middle managers are often highly involved in this phase, working directly with end users to adopt the innovation and providing feedback to the sponsor and implementation team on what is and is not working. In addition, the sponsor, along with the governance body, often decides which **improvements** will move forward in future iterations of the implementation.

Finally, the sponsor should aim to finish strong, not fade away. She should remain engaged in the effort throughout the **Maintain** phase, to ensure sufficient transition planning is undertaken and resources are secured to sustain the innovation. The governance body often plays a role in approving plans and resources for the transition and signing off on final performance reports related to the change implementation.

STARTER STEPS: Leadership

Leaders in implementation come from all levels and functions in the organization. However, three roles provide explicit direction and support for the effort: the sponsor, governance body, and middle managers. Individuals filling those roles should be sure to:

1. **Clarify the vision, direction, and goals of the change.** The sponsor should work with others, at minimum members of the governance body, to sharpen the vision and develop the goals of the implementation. Middle managers are often called on to champion the change locally, including translating the broader vision of the change into messages and plans that are relevant to their staff.

2. **Establish procedures and processes to support your work.** The sponsor and implementation lead or project manager should clarify up front how they will work together and what is most important to them. Additionally, the sponsor and implementation lead should engage with the governance body and representative middle managers to establish a schedule of governance meetings, clarify norms, and other procedures. This work may also include defining the governance framework for the implementation.

3. **Start communicating and don't stop.** The sponsor is integrally involved in explaining the need, vision, and goals of the implementation. Additionally, in both formal and informal ways, others in leadership roles are often involved in change communications. Aligning on key messages up front can help to avoid confusion. And remember, actions speak louder than words. Leaders at all levels should be aware that how they ask for input and respond to questions, concerns, and challenges will have as much impact as any presentations they give.

EXPERT TIPS

Specify how much time leaders will invest in the implementation. Saying "I'll be there whenever you need me" may seem like a reassuring statement, but it's not realistic. Clarifying expectations for the time leaders can devote to the effort can help the team to identify the most impactful ways to use this time.

Identify things that only a leader can do and do them. All those in change leadership positions should aim to complement, not duplicate, other roles.

Be clear about your doubts and blind spots. Leaders need to have confidence in the change, but not necessarily everything about it. Sponsors should aim to create an environment where leaders feel comfortable voicing their concerns so that they can be addressed. Additionally, leaders can aim to identify their blind spots by asking stakeholders: What should we be asking you that we're not? What should we be paying more attention to and why? What do you think we are we missing?

Notes

1. This case was adapted from U.S. Department of Health and Human Services Office of the Inspector General. (2016). Healthcare.gov: CMS management of the Federal Marketplace. A case study. (DHHS Publication No. OEI-06-14-00350). Washington, DC: U.S. Government Printing Office. Retrieved from https://oig.hhs.gov/oei/reports/oei-06-14-00350.pdf and Thorp, F. (2013, October 31). Only 6 able to sign up on healthcare.gov's first day, documents show. Retrieved from https://www.nbcnews.com/news/other/only-6-able-sign-healthcare-govs-first-day-documents-show-f8C11509571
2. For more on leadership styles during organizational change see ten Have, S., ten Have, W., Huijsmans, A. B., & Otto, M. (2016). *Reconsidering Change Management: Applying evidence-based insights in change management practice*. Routledge.
3. There are many frameworks outlining change leadership competencies, none of which can be called "the best." For a review of research on the role of leaders in change see Ford, J. D., & Ford, L. W. (2012). The leadership of organization change: A view from recent empirical evidence. In *Research in Organizational Change and Development* (pp. 1-36). Emerald Group Publishing Limited. doi: 10.1108/S0897-3016(2012)0000020004. For a discussion of one competency framework see Battilana, J., Gilmartin, M., Sengul, M., Pache, A. C., & Alexander, J. A. (2010). Leadership competencies for implementing planned organizational change. *The Leadership Quarterly*, 21(3), 422-438. doi: 10.1016/j.leaqua.2010.03.007
4. For more information on this aspect of the sponsor role, refer to work on transformational change leadership, such as Heifetz, R. A., & Linsky, M. (2002). *Leadership on the line: Staying alive through the dangers of leading*. Boston: Harvard Business School Press, and Kotter, J. P. (2007). Leading change: Why transformation efforts fail. *Harvard Business Review*, 73(2).Retrieved from https://hbr.org/2007/01/leading-change-why-transformation-efforts-fail
5. Achilles Armenakis and colleagues suggest those impacted by an organizational change are influenced by five beliefs. Among them are the beliefs that the change is the "right" one and that the organization is capable of implementing it. See Armenakis, A. A., & Harris, S. G. (2009). Reflections: Our journey in organizational change research and practice. Journal of Change Management, 9(2), 127-142. doi:10.1080/14697010902879079

6. For a discussion of the links between fairness and change see ten Have, S., ten Have, W., Huijsmans, A. B., & Otto, M. (2016). *Reconsidering Change Management: Applying evidence-based insights in change management practice.* Routledge. Related to building trust see Mayer, R. C., Davis, J. H., & Schoorman, F. D. (1995). An integrative model of organizational trust. *Academy of Management Review,* 20(3), 709-734. doi: 10.5465/AMR.1995.9508080335. Finally, Achilles Armenakis and colleagues suggest that those impacted by a change are influenced by five beliefs, one of which is whether or not the change will be beneficial to them. See Armenakis, A. A., & Harris, S. G. (2009). Reflections: Our journey in organizational change research and practice. *Journal of Change Management,* 9(2), 127-142. doi:10.1080/14697010902879079

7. See Heifetz, R. A., & Laurie, D. L. (1997). The Work of Leadership. *Harvard Business Review,* 75, 124-134. Retrieved from https://hbr.org/2001/12/the-work-of-leadership

8. There are many frameworks that aim to meaningfully organize change leadership competencies. I draw these three — communication, mobilization, and evaluation — from the framework provided by Battilana, J., Gilmartin, M., Sengul, M., Pache, A. C., & Alexander, J. A. (2010). Leadership competencies for implementing planned organizational change. *The Leadership Quarterly,* 21(3), 422-438. doi:10.1016/j.leaqua.2010.03.007. For more discussion of middle manager roles and how to support middle managers in change see Balogun, J. (2003). From Blaming the Middle to Harnessing its Potential: Creating Change Intermediaries. *British Journal of Management,* 14(1), 69-83. doi:10.1111/1467-8551.00266 and Heyden, M. L. M., Fourné, S. P. L., Koene, B. A. S., Werkman, R., & Ansari, S. S. (2017). Rethinking 'Top-Down' and 'Bottom-Up' Roles of Top and Middle Managers in Organizational Change: Implications for Employee Support. *Journal of Management Studies,* 54(7), 961-985. doi:10.1111/joms.12258

9. For more on the "emotional balancing" role of middle managers see Huy, Q. N. (2002). Emotional Balancing of Organizational Continuity and Radical Change: The Contribution of Middle Managers. *Administrative Science Quarterly,* 47(1), 31. doi:10.2307/3094890

END USERS

Change can't happen without them

An Inside Job: Staff members challenge a new banking program

In 2012, FINCA, an organization that provides the poor with access to basic financial services, launched a new agency banking program. Bank agents are small business owners that partner with FINCA to augment its branch locations. These agents conduct financial transactions that customers cannot complete through mobile banking, such as making cash deposits. In the early days of the implementation of the agency program, the organization ran into a critical challenge — branch staff and management were not fully aligned or supportive of the program's goals. Branch staff members felt their jobs may be threatened by the program and actively discouraged customers from using agent locations. Managers did not feel accountable for the success of the program.

To combat this challenge, leaders of the agency banking program continually articulated to branch staff the goals and benefits of the program. They emphasized how the program supported the viability and financial health of the greater organization. They also included branch staff in some aspects of program decision-making, including asking for their help in identifying agent locations, as well as in training new agents. To better engage managers, key progress measures for the agency program were identified and integrated into an existing set of metrics used to monitor the business.[1]

In any implementation, there is a core group of people that will adopt or use the change that is being implemented. In this book, I refer to them as end users. Often these folks are drawn from front-line staff in an organization, but employees at all levels may have an end user role to play.

In this chapter, we'll discuss how to engage with end users to support the success of your implementation.

Your primary job is to support end users

In very tangible terms, you are dependent on end users for the success of the implementation. If people don't adopt what you are implementing, you can't achieve results. Period.

When implementing change, you don't always make life easy for end users, at least not in the short-term. Usually, you add to their workload, asking them to go beyond their day-to-day responsibilities. You make their day more complicated, if not harder, longer, and more stressful.

Recognizing this, instead of prioritizing the demands, ideas, and desires of top management or the implementation team — which is relatively easy to do — consider prioritizing the needs of end users. Or at least take pains to ensure the perspectives of end users are given equal weight.

In doing so, it's important to understand that the support required by end users may take a variety of forms. Some research indicates that an interplay of multiple factors — ability (knowledge, skills), motivation (beliefs, goals), and opportunity (resources, environment) — may account for whether people change or not.[2] Therefore, truly assisting end users may require efforts beyond building awareness and skills (ability) through training. It may also require you to address other factors, such as conflicting beliefs or goals (motivation) or resource constraints (opportunity), that may impact end users' adoption of a change.

Be sure you know who your end users are

The end user group always includes core users. These are the people who most naturally and directly integrate the innovation in their day-to-day work. However, you should expect that end user roles will be diverse. Looking beyond the obvious players can help you to avoid gaps in your outreach and support.

For example, a manager may not have a day-to-day role in adopting the innovation but may be called on to analyze, discuss, or react to data that are available as a result of the implementation, putting her in an end user role.

Keep in mind, end users are part of a broader constituency called stakeholders, which we discuss in the next chapter. However, unlike stakeholders in general, end users don't simply aim to influence the implementation. Rather, end users have a specific function to perform or are required to take a defined set of actions to adopt the innovation.

Identify connection points

As mentioned in the previous chapter on implementation teams, you may benefit from assigning members of that team to act as liaisons to groups of end users. Even if you don't name such points of contact formally, the implementation team should map out its connection points to end users. If, based on this mapping, you find you are a few degrees of separation from end users, discuss how you will mitigate the risks of misinformation or confusion caused by this distance.

For instance, you may rely on managers to support and train their staff, rather than doing so directly. Providing managers with key messages, presentation materials, handouts, and other support items can help to increase the likelihood they are communicating accurate information about the innovation. This is more work for you. But, it's more efficient to concentrate that effort among a few members of the implementation team and more effective than just asking the managers to do their best.

Additionally, if you don't have regular, direct contact with end users, you may want to observe or shadow a few groups during the execution phase, to gather learning and better understand their challenges. Observation will help you to identify barriers, enhance your support, and inform improvements to the design of the innovation. Through observation, you can also create and distribute a catalog of practices and ideas drawn directly from end users. It's been my experience that people love to learn about practices used by others, but rarely ask for or share such knowledge on their own.

Finally, whenever you are involved in shadowing or observation, it's important that the process is not perceived as punitive. Your objective is to learn and improve the process, not to evaluate or judge individuals or teams.

Create input and feedback loops

In addition to identifying formal liaisons or undertaking observation, you'll want to create opportunities for end users to provide input and feedback to the implementation team throughout the lifespan of the implementation. (The degree of engagement that is appropriate will vary from change to change. For more on tailoring your approach to your context, see the Context chapter.)

Such engagement can include things like surveys, one-on-one or small group interviews, and design sessions or workshops. I recommend using a variety of different methods. I also recommend following the golden rules of engagement:

- **Don't ask for what you won't use.** If you know that something isn't going to change, don't spend a lot of

time getting ideas from people on how to change it.
- **Always close the loop.** If you ask for feedback or input, summarize it and communicate it back to those who provided it, along with information about how you will use their ideas going forward.

As best you can, give end users opportunities to directly interact with the innovation to inform their input, perhaps even through a pilot. What people *think* will be a challenge or a resource is often entirely different from what *is actually* a challenge or resource. (For more on pilots and testing, see the chapter on Phases.)

If the implementation team needs feedback from people beyond its reach, the executive sponsor may be able to open doors or even to meet with these people to gather their feedback.

Finally, be sure to regularly update end users on progress — what you've learned, how it's going, and what's coming next. A 2017 survey by McKinsey, a consulting firm, found that front-line staff consider access to progress information to be an important form of engagement. Much more so, in fact, than managers or executives do.[3]

Balance autonomy and integrity

Autonomy relates to a person's perceived level of control over how, when, and where she performs her job activities. An array of research indicates that autonomy is strongly linked with staff commitment, satisfaction, and other behaviors that support organizational change.[4]

However, autonomy given to end users to adjust the innovation needs to be balanced with support for the integrity of the effort. Integrity is one of the "Three I's of Implementation" discussed in Part II; it requires that you ensure the effectiveness factors of the innovation, also known as core components, are consistently implemented.

Take, for example, the experience of several community-based substance abuse prevention programs.[5] In these implementations, teachers delivering the programs had some degree of autonomy. They could decide if they would use large groups, small groups, or individual sessions to engage participants in program material. To support their work, some teachers used local data on substance use, rather than national data. Some also created additional worksheets or tests to support the learning of key concepts among their students. These adjustments did not impinge on the integrity of the effort. However, when teachers omitted certain modules due to unfamiliarity, discomfort, or a lack of time, this was found to impact the integrity of the innovation.

While this example comes from a community-based program, the lesson applies to other business settings as well. For example, staff or managers may decide to skip steps in a process or apply a new policy in ways that were not intended, either of which could reduce the integrity of the implementation.

View end users as advocates, as well as adopters

Your primary focus may be to help end users adopt the innovation. However, you should also consider preparing end users to be informed explainers, if not full-blown advocates of the implementation, during interactions with their peers, customers, vendors, or partners.

In some cases, you can do this by adhering to the first principle mentioned in this chapter. The simpler you make the change for end users, the less likely they are to be frustrated with it, to complain to others about it, or to experience reduced productivity that impacts customers or other stakeholders.

You can also consider preparing end users to speak about the change should someone ask. Talking points outlining what the innovation is, how it will benefit these stakeholders, and the main differences the stakeholders may experience should be sufficient. You needn't get into the sausage making.

Phases and End Users

Plan to engage and inform end users throughout the lifespan of the implementation. This means engagement should start well before you ask end users to adopt the change. During the **Decide** phase, end users can help to inform the selection and adaptation of the innovation you will implement. During the **Prepare** phase, end users can provide feedback and input during design workshops or testing.

Of course, during the **Execute** phase, you will engage end users to help you identify not only issues and difficulties, but also how to overcome them in the **Improve** phase. Finally, be sure to continue to engage with end users throughout the **Maintain** phase. It's likely that end users will require some level of support in the long-term, although less than during the early stages of adoption. Be sure end users know where to go for assistance as the implementation transitions to normal operations.

STARTER STEPS: End Users

End users are integral to the success of any implementation. If people don't adopt what you are implementing, you can't achieve results. To effectively support and engage with end users, be sure to:

1. **Identify groups of end users and the unique needs of each group.** Unlike stakeholders in general, who may have an interest in the effort or aim to influence it, end users are required to fulfill a function or take a defined action to adopt the change.

2. **Develop an engagement plan**, indicating how you will interact with each end user group in each phase of the implementation. If you aren't planning on engaging with specific groups of end users, be clear about why. Finally, remember that engagement should start well before training.

3. **Organize your implementation team to support end users.** Clarify and communicate how you'll provide support to end users before they ask.

EXPERT TIPS

Include an agenda item on end user engagement during regular meetings of the implementation team and governance body. Challenge your team to answer the question: How can we make things 10% easier for end users?

Make end user engagement as hands-on as possible. Test prototypes, use pilots, or organize site visits to organizations using the innovation to help end users experience it first hand. Input and feedback about actual experiences, rather than assumptions, are usually more valuable.

Eliminate the black hole of feedback. Whenever you formally engage with end users, be sure to close the loop by providing a summary of what you heard and offering next steps. Regularly update end users on how the implementation is progressing.

Notes

1. This case was adapted from Were, N., & Lin, H. (2017). *The long road to branchless banking 2017* (Rep.) Retrieved from https://www.finca.org/about-finca/finca-publications/case-studies/long-road-branchless-banking/
2. See, for example, Stouten, J., Rousseau, D., & De Cremer, D. (2018). Successful organizational change: Integrating the management practice and scholarly literatures. *Academy of Management Annals*, 12(2), 752-788. doi:10.5465/annals.2016.0095 or Armitage, C. J., & Conner, M. (2001). Efficacy of the theory of planned behaviour: A meta-analytic review. *British Journal of Social Psychology*, 40(4), 471-499. doi: 10.1348/014466601164939
3. See Maor, D., & Reich, A. (2017). The People Power of Transformations. Retrieved from https://www.mckinsey.com/business-functions/organization/our-insights/the-people-power-of-transformations
4. See, for example, Marinova, S. V., Peng, C., Lorinkova, N., Van Dyne, L., & Chiaburu, D. (2015). Change-oriented behavior: A meta-analysis of individual and job design predictors. *Journal of Vocational Behavior, 88*, 104-120. doi: 10.1016/j.jvb.2015.02.006
5. This example was adapted from Fagan, A. A., Hanson, K., Hawkins, J. D., & Arthur, M. W. (2008). Bridging science to practice: Achieving prevention program implementation fidelity in the Community Youth Development Study. *American Journal of Community Psychology, 41*(3-4), 235-249. doi: 10.1007/s10464-008-9176-x

STAKEHOLDERS

Influencers, customers, and more

Absence makes the heart grow fonder

"When the new Coke came out, I borrowed my friend's pick-up and went to a club store and bought three pallets of regular Coke. It took two trips to get the Coke home. I had enough Coke to last me through the crisis, but I had to repair the floor in my spare bedroom — because of all the weight, the floor had sunk. It was well worth it."[1]

In 1985, when The Coca-Cola Company replaced its signature beverage with a new formula, it wanted to shake things up. The company had been losing market share for over 15 years, and the demand for cola products, in general, was lagging. However, as the company discovered when it launched the so-called New Coke, Americans may have been buying less Coke, but they had no desire to see the drink change.

The response to the new offering was nothing less than outrage. Complaints were immediate, with the company soon fielding 1,500 consumer calls a day — more than three times the normal call volume. This was surprising given that 200,000 consumers had preferred New Coke in blind taste tests conducted before the product launch. However, the people had spoken. Within three months, the company responded to popular sentiment and put original Coke back on the shelves. New Coke is no longer available in the United States.[2]

Understanding what motivates stakeholders and how they may react to change is tricky, but learning to do so is essential for implementers. In this chapter, we discuss how to identify and understand stakeholder perspectives, decide which are most critical, and use this information to inform engagement planning. We conclude the chapter with a discussion of common stakeholder challenges and opportunities, and what to do when you face them.

What Is a Stakeholder?

Definitions of stakeholders vary, but in general, stakeholders are the people who are impacted by or who can affect your implementation.[3] By this definition, all of the roles discussed in Part V are stakeholders — the implementation team, sponsor, governance body, and end users are all impacted by or have the ability to influence the implementation.

The tactics and tools outlined in this chapter apply to all stakeholders, but are offered with the specific intention of helping you to identify and understand the perspectives of less apparent influencers and impacted groups.

For instance, let's go back to the case of the California class-size reduction effort discussed at the start of the book. The stakeholders of that implementation included district administrators (implementation team); school administrators and teachers (end users); as well as statewide officials including the governor, legislators, and representatives of the Department of Education (leadership). However, the implementation also had other stakeholders. These included students who were affected by changes in the classroom; parents who had opinions about the instructional environment created by the implementation; and education experts who may have been interested in learning from the experience in California or who had expectations about it.[4]

Perspectives on Stakeholder Engagement

Engaging with stakeholders, who may have diverse or even conflicting perspectives, interests, and attitudes, takes a certain level of skill and open-mindedness. If you view stakeholders as a potential threat to your authority or knowledge, it's unlikely you will engage with them effectively. Likewise, superficial or paternalistic engagement efforts will be easily identified as inauthentic.

The evidence about engagement in implementation is somewhat mixed. Some research indicates it's beneficial to take an open, problem-solving mindset when interacting with stakeholders.[5] Other scholars suggest a more nuanced approach that is informed by the specifics of your situation.

For instance, if there is a need for new or different expertise, a desire to build commitment, or a problem without an apparent owner, this may be a scenario well-suited to stakeholder engagement and participation. However, when expertise exists, a decision has already been made, or no one cares about the issue, you may want to limit engagement efforts.[6]

The level of interest stakeholders have in the implementation, as well as their power to influence it, will also shape how you interact with them and respond to their ideas and concerns. The tools outlined in the remainder of this chapter will help you to identify the most critical stakeholders, as well as tailor your engagement efforts appropriately for different stakeholder groups.

Regardless of the strategy you use, it is essential to be consistent and transparent about it.[7] For that reason, you'll want to agree in principle on your engagement approach with your leadership as well as key members of your implementation team. Consider having such conversations at the outset of your effort, as well as after you have undertaken a stakeholder analysis, which we discuss next.

Analysis and Action: Tools to Use

Analysis: Identifying and understanding your stakeholders

The time and effort your implementation team and leadership invest in better understanding your stakeholders — who they are, what's important to them, and which among them are the most critical — may have value beyond any concrete plan produced from such analysis.[8] Frank discussions about stakeholders can help you to see gaps you didn't realize were there, identify hidden sources of power, and perhaps even recognize that some people who have outsize voices have little influence. For this reason, when engaging your team and others in such discussions, I encourage you to focus as much on the process — rich and honest conversations — as on the end product.

Who are your stakeholders?

There are many tools that can help you identify stakeholders, most of which encourage you to start off by brainstorming a list of all potential stakeholders.[9] Questions that may assist you in generating such a list include:

- Who will be asked to do something specific during the implementation?
- Who will be directly impacted by, but not directly involved in adopting the change?
- Who might be indirectly impacted?
- Who may not be directly involved, but is still able to influence the effort?
- Who will feel challenged or threatened?
- Who will see or feel benefits or advantages?
- Who wants you to succeed?
- Who wants you to fail (or go away)?

This exercise may be most useful when you identify stakeholders with some degree of specificity. For example, rather than using a broad stakeholder category such as "divisions" or "regions" break it down further to pinpoint the relevant groups within the division or region. This could be at an individual level, (e.g., the VP of Finance, Director of Asia Operations) or related to specific units within the division or region.[10]

Which stakeholders matter most and why?

Effective stakeholder engagement planning requires more than an extensive list of stakeholders. A common second step involves categorizing the list based on key factors, thereby distinguishing the stakeholders that are most relevant. You cannot do this effectively unless you can see the implementation from the perspective of each stakeholder. If you lack familiarity with some stakeholder groups, you'll want to get input from those with knowledge of these groups.

One of the most widely used tools to categorize stakeholders is the Power and Interest grid devised by Fran Ackermann and Colin Eden. This grid helps you to evaluate the level of interest various stakeholders have in the implementation as well as their relative power to impact it.[11] Other tools focus this analysis on different combinations of factors such as commitment/knowledge, support/influence, or importance/attitude. I summarize these various approaches in Figure 15.[12]

You can use the matrix to chart the position of each stakeholder based on how they rate on different factors. In general, those stakeholders positioned in the top right quadrant are the most critical and those in the bottom left the least.

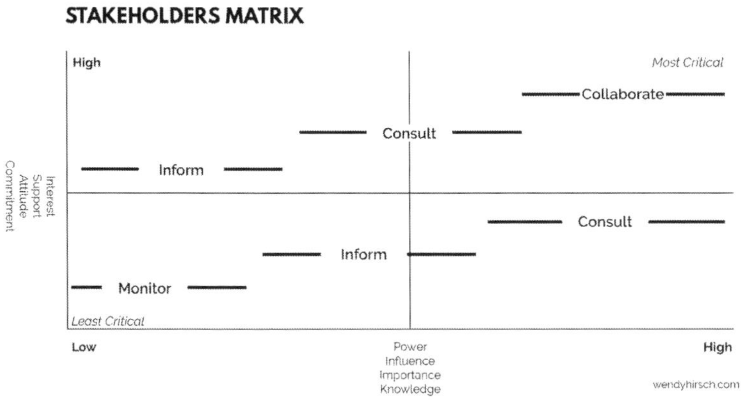

STAKEHOLDERS MATRIX

```
High                                              Most Critical
                                        ——— Collaborate ———
                               ——— Consult ———
Interest        ——— Inform ———
Support
Attitude
Commitment                                   ——— Consult ———
                           ——— Inform ———
             ——— Monitor ———
Least Critical
Low             Power                                    High
                Influence
                Importance
                Knowledge                    wendyhirsch.com
```

Figure 15 – Stakeholders Matrix

However, what the quadrants indicate is nuanced. It will depend on the factors you put on the x- and y-axes and if you add a third dimension, such as whether the stakeholder's interest or commitment is positive or negative.

Assigning stakeholders to various quadrants not only provides insight into individual stakeholders, but also potential coalitions that can be encouraged or discouraged. The process can also help to build agreement among the team about who counts as a "key" stakeholder. However, such categorization will only be useful if you take action based on it.

Action planning: Tailoring your engagement efforts

Stakeholder engagement relates to what you do to share ideas and information with stakeholders, as well as how you respond to their input and concerns. For instance, do you acknowledge their opinions, incorporate them to some degree into your plans, or take them as directives?

Rather than thinking about engagement as an all-or-nothing affair, it can be helpful to consider it as running along a spectrum.

This spectrum may involve monitoring (or doing nothing) at the low end, continuing through to information provision and consultation in the middle, with full collaboration at the high end.

You can overlay the spectrum of engagement actions on the matrix described previously. Doing so can provide a broad indication of the type of engagement activities you will use with stakeholders depending on their location on the matrix, as illustrated in Figure 15. After the matrix has been populated you can translate it into a simple engagement plan, which might include things such as the stakeholders, their level of priority, how you'll engage with them, and who on your team is on point to do so.

Examples: Engagement in Action

While it's important to analyze your stakeholders and plan your engagement strategies, such tactics may feel removed from the reality of interactions you are likely to have. For that reason, in the remainder of this chapter, I share some common challenges and opportunities I have experienced when working with stakeholders and tips on what to do if you face them.

CHALLENGES

Scope Creep

A defined scope of work provides useful boundaries for the implementation effort. It helps everyone develop shared expectations about what is and is not changing. Additionally, a defined scope or scale of change allows the implementation team to move forward with confidence that the task at hand is manageable given the resources available. Scope creep happens when stakeholders want the implementation to address their challenges, even when these challenges are not aligned with the stated goals of the effort. They want to expand the effort to meet their needs; however, for the reasons noted above, scope changes should not be undertaken lightly.

A practical response strategy for scope creep starts with acknowledgment. Recognize, rather than trying to diminish, the validity of the issues raised by these stakeholders. However, do so while reiterating — privately and publicly — that their problem lies outside the purpose and desired results of the current implementation. In such situations, it can be tempting to avoid confrontation by responding with something like, "We can consider that," or "We'll look into that." However, if you won't consider it because the scope has already been decided, you should say so.

Second, encourage your sponsor and members of the governance body to publicly communicate their decisions related to the purpose, objectives, and scope of the effort and hold firm to them. It may also be necessary to have them help you actively manage stakeholders who are advocating for changes.

Do it my way (but don't ask me to do anything)

Some stakeholders are looking for control without the related responsibility. They want to have technical input on, or even authority to decide, what or how you implement. However, they avoid taking a formal role in the implementation.

This is particularly problematic when the implementation falls under the broad interests and functional responsibility of multiple managers who may have different technical expertise or perspectives. Ideally, in this situation, the managers come together and identify where they need to collaborate related to the implementation and where they can continue to operate independently. In my role as implementation lead, I always try to facilitate such collaboration, and it's wonderful when the managers play along!

However, some managers like things fuzzy. They offer advice and opinions but resist undertaking the formal collaboration necessary to produce a unified way forward. This contributes to confusion among end users and ensures technical issues are continually revisited throughout the life of the effort. Unfortunately, this situation is not rare and the challenge is not always solvable.

However, we can draw a lesson from this example that has broad applicability — although others may prefer to keep things vague, you can make every effort to ensure things within your control are explicit.

You can be clear about membership on the implementation team and governance body. You can be clear about the sources of technical expertise you are drawing on to guide the design of the innovation and how you are implementing it. Finally, you can be clear about the degree to which you will use input from opinionated, but commitment-averse stakeholders.

I can wait you out

When your change implementation is viewed as a threat, you can expect some people to actively and overtly challenge it. Others, who can be far more problematic, will support your efforts in words, but not deeds. These people may meet with you or even offer to partner with you, but never take the actions necessary to adopt the innovation. I have identified a common belief among such stakeholders. It is this — they can wait you out. They believe the implementation will eventually fail, and they will be wiser for not having participated in it.

This belief may be quite sensible, especially if these stakeholders have seen similar efforts fail in the past, or if the organization has a reputation for constant change.

With such stakeholders, who often are end users or their managers, I find extensive discussions are not particularly useful. They will be pleasant and agreeable conversations, but not productive. However, there are tactics that may be beneficial, all of which require a certain amount of patience. These include:

- **Demonstrate tangible progress.** You need to prove that you are not failing and that the effort is moving forward. Similarly, it can help to ask the leadership of your effort to communicate the organization's continued commitment to it.
- **Show that you know who is participating in the implementation and who is not.** It's common when giving progress updates to a governance body to mention adoption rates. (Your monitoring and measurement efforts will be essential to enable this.) Eventually, leaders will ask about the partners, teams, or departments that are not yet on board and follow up with them. Alternatively, you can highlight and celebrate success stories among the peer group of laggards; competition can be motivating.
- **Ask leaders to intervene.** In many cases, after you have tried the tactics mentioned above, people who have consciously opted out will begin to question their rationale for doing so. I have had people tell me, "I thought you would just go away…but it's been over a year, and you're still here. So, we need to start doing this." However, if they don't have a change of heart, it is likely time to engage your leadership. I don't recommend strong leadership intervention at the start because implementation is usually a long-term affair. You need to choose your battles and identify the challenges that time itself might help to overcome.

OPPORTUNITIES

Seek out and exploit common interests

Most implementations aim to embed changes that are not completely novel. They may formalize some variant of practices or ideas that have been active in various parts of the organization for a while. At the very least, there are likely to be people who will say, "I've been talking about doing this for years!"

Don't assume that such people are already formally involved in your effort. Seek them out and work hard to make them part of the broader coalition supporting your implementation. Above all, do not ignore them or their prior contributions.

Share the spotlight

Although you will probably designate a specific individual to act as the spokesperson for your implementation, don't be shy about passing the microphone around. This can be literal, by having early adopters or those involved in pilots share their experiences in town halls, videos, or training sessions. But this can also be more informal.

If you've created a diverse implementation team, consider giving all team members some communications responsibilities, particularly with their respective constituencies. These team members may also be helpful in identifying peers who are willing to share their ideas and support. Be prepared to ask these people to speak up. Although we'd like to believe everyone will love our effort so much they have no problem standing up for it, speaking up takes energy and can feel risky to some. Be proactive to encourage positive voices.

Phases and Stakeholders

During the **Decide** phase, when developing the purpose and desired outcomes of the effort, work with your sponsor and others to identify critical stakeholders who need to be involved in this activity. Engage them upfront to avoid rework or confusion later on. During the **Prepare** phase, facilitate discussions with your implementation team, sponsor, and governance body to identify stakeholders and plan your engagement strategies.

During the **Execute** phase, you'll put your stakeholder engagement plan into action and monitor and respond to stakeholder issues that arise as the innovation is rolled out. You may need to adjust your engagement plan based on learning from initial implementation efforts or changing requirements; you'll make such updates during the **Improve** phase. Document your learning about stakeholders and identify ongoing engagement that may be required when the innovation is transitioned to ongoing operations during the **Maintain** phase.

STARTER STEPS: Stakeholders

Stakeholders include anyone who is impacted by, or who influences, your implementation. Effective stakeholder engagement requires you to identify the stakeholders who matter the most and plan appropriate ways to interact with them. To do so, you may wish to:

1. **Develop a shared perspective on stakeholder engagement.** As a matter of principle, how open are you to diverse ideas? How much energy will you invest in addressing stakeholder concerns? Ensure you are transparent about your approach and that all of those involved in the implementation apply it consistently.

2. **Identify your stakeholders, their interests, and their relative power.** Do this through a focused conversation with your team and leadership. If your team lacks familiarity with some stakeholder groups, be sure to invite those who are familiar with them to take part in the discussion.

3. **Plan appropriate action.** Once you have identified stakeholders, plan your engagement activities. Appropriate actions will run along a spectrum from monitoring to deep collaboration.

EXPERT TIPS

Keep it simple, but don't skip it. Simplicity may help you to overcome one common challenge in stakeholder analysis – many people don't want to "waste time" talking about stakeholders. If your sponsor, team, or others resist having a meeting solely focused on stakeholder identification and analysis, get creative. Integrate the topic as a discussion point in interviews with leaders or advisors, or develop a straw man stakeholder list and analysis, and gather feedback on it.

Keep it alive. To maintain an appropriate focus on stakeholders throughout the implementation consider integrating measures of stakeholder engagement into progress updates or including it as a regular agenda item in governance meetings.

Be specific! Be choosy! The more granularly you identify stakeholders, the more likely you are to understand what's truly important to them and how much they might influence the implementation. Once you do this, focus your engagement efforts on a critical handful of stakeholders. Remember, less is more. You are not aiming to engage or please everyone.

Aim to understand. Some people shy away from stakeholder analysis and engagement because they feel it is manipulative. An alternative view is that it is a sign of respect, demonstrating a strong desire to understand and work with others. I advocate that you act in ways that align with the latter perspective.

Notes

1. Coca-Cola fans share their stories. (2012, January 1). Retrieved from http://www.coca-colacompany.com/stories/coca-cola-stories-new-coke
2. The real story of New Coke. (2012, November 14). Retrieved from http://www.coca-colacompany.com/stories/coke-lore-new-coke
3. For a discussion of the various definitions of stakeholders and the implications of each, see Bryson, J. M. (2004). What to do when stakeholders matter: Stakeholder identification and analysis techniques. *Public Management Review, 6*(1), 21-53. doi:10.1080/14719030410001675722
4. For a full review of this case, see Bohrnstedt, G. W. & Stecher, B. M. (Eds.). (2002). What we have learned about class size reduction. Sacramento, CA: California Department of Education. Retrieved from http://www.classize.org/techreport/CSRYear4_final.pdf
5. See, for example, Pasmore, W. A., & Fagans, M. R. (1992). Participation, individual development, and organizational change: A review and synthesis. *Journal of Management, 18*(2), 375-397. doi:10.1177/014920639201800208; Sloan, P. (2009). Redefining stakeholder engagement: From control to collaboration. *Journal of Corporate Citizenship, 36*, 25-40. Retrieved from http://www.ingentaconnect.com/content/glbj/jcc/2009/00002009/00000036/art00005?crawler=true; or Beierle, T. C. (2002). The quality of stakeholder-based decisions. *Risk Analysis, 22*(4), 739-749. doi:10.1111/0272-4332.00065
6. For more on taking a situational approach to staff participation in change see Kanter, R. M. (1982). Dilemmas of managing participation. *Organizational Dynamics, 11*(1), 5-27. doi:10.1016/0090-2616(82)90039-0. For a broader discussion on managerial approaches to stakeholder engagement in implementation, see Nutt, P. C. (1986). Tactics of implementation. *Academy of Management Journal, 29*(2), 230-261. doi:10.2307/256187
7. For a discussion see Bowen, F., Newenham-Kahindi, A., & Herremans, I. (2010). When suits meet roots: The antecedents and consequences of community engagement strategy. *Journal of Business Ethics, 95*(2), 297-318. doi:10.1007/s10551-009-0360-1
8. See Ackermann, F., & Eden, C. (2011). Strategic management of stakeholders: Theory and practice. *Long Range Planning, 44*(3), 179-196. doi:10.1016/j.lrp.2010.08.001
9. For an overview, see Bryson, J. M. (2004). What to do when stake-

holders matter: Stakeholder identification and analysis techniques. *Public Management Review, 6*(1), 21-53. doi:10.1080/14719030410001675722

10. See the discussion on disaggregation and uniqueness in Ackermann, F., & Eden, C. (2011). Strategic management of stakeholders: Theory and practice. *Long Range Planning, 44*(3), 179-196. doi:10.1016/j.lrp.2010.08.001

11. See Ackermann, F., & Eden, C. (2011). Strategic management of stakeholders: Theory and practice. *Long Range Planning, 44*(3), 179-196. doi:10.1016/j.lrp.2010.08.001

12. This grid integrates a variety of approaches to stakeholder analysis for illustrative purposes. For a review of multiple methods see Stakeholder matrix — key matrices for stakeholder analysis. (n.d.). Retrieved from https://www.stakeholdermap.com/stakeholder-matrix.html#dragan

PART VI: WHERE

In this section, we investigate how internal and external factors can impact your implementation and how to adapt your efforts to meet the unique needs of your context.

CONTEXT

Where you implement matters

Same innovation, different implementation strategies

In the 1990s, two companies, one an elevator company in China, the other an Australian firm working in the petroleum industry, both successfully concluded major ERP system implementations. When staff at each organization were interviewed about the factors they felt were most critical to their success, what they highlighted was surprising for its variety.

Staff at both organizations felt top management support and a diverse implementation team were essential. However, the Chinese firm highlighted the importance of vendor support and data integrity, while the Australian team didn't mention these. This may be because the Chinese firm did not have in-house technical skills to draw on, but the Australian firm did. The Chinese firm had also had difficulty with its data quality in the past, while the Australian firm felt it had high-quality legacy data to work with.

In contrast, employees at the Australian firm tended to emphasize change management and having full-time internal staff dedicated to the effort, while these were not mentioned by the Chinese interviewees. Perhaps due to norms of their national culture, the Chinese staff members perceived the change as a given. Therefore, they prioritized training and helping employees understand what they needed to do and put less emphasis on efforts to convince employees that the change was a good idea.

In the Australian firm, employees were more accustomed to questioning changes; the firm felt it was important to develop change champions among the staff who would consistently advocate for the effort. In addition, the Australian firm used vendor support only on a part-time basis at the outset of the effort. Therefore, the availability of in-house staff to help with the implementation was critical in ways that were not relevant to the Chinese implementation, which relied on vendor support throughout. As these cases demonstrate, some aspects of implementation may be similar regardless of context, but others are likely to be quite different for reasons related to the culture, capacity, and past experiences of the organization and its employees.[1]

The innovation you implement, what you emphasize in your approach, and how you interact with stakeholders are all aspects of your implementation that will be influenced by your context. Context is the environment in which you are implementing. It includes internal factors, which can differ from team to team as well as from organization to organization. Context also encompasses external factors related to the industry, geographic location, or even economic conditions in which you or those impacted by the implementation are working.

Although research on implementation consistently calls out the importance of context in general, many implementations are studied and documented without explicitly noting contextual factors.[2] Therefore, we know context matters, but we can't say definitely which contextual factors are likely to make a difference in *all* implementations. However, it is possible to identify the contextual factors that are most likely to matter to *your* implementation.

In this chapter, we review how to identify critical contextual factors and how to use them to inform your implementation approach.

You Don't Know What You Don't Know

It's essential not to take context for granted or make general assumptions about it based on the perspectives of a single constituency. Be sure to enlist a diverse group to provide insights into your context, to avoid blind spots and uncover unique viewpoints.

To illustrate this, let's consider the experience of a team of coders who were brought in to fix the healthcare.gov website after it failed within hours of its launch. (This site was part of the implementation of the Affordable Care Act in the United States and was meant to serve as the primary conduit through which many citizens would buy health insurance plans made available through this law.)

The turnaround team of IT specialists hailed from the likes of Google, as well as various startups. Tools that they assumed would be available to support their work — such as messaging software, agile project management methods, or cloud-based data centers — were not. The lack of these tools not only impacted their productivity but also the performance of the site they were trying to fix.

However, the reason these tools were not being used wasn't necessarily what the tech team anticipated. It wasn't a simple lack of awareness or low levels of tech-savviness amongst government employees. It was also due to the high stakes nature of government work. People were slower to try new things because the impact of mistakes or failure was more significant in government than, say, when developing a food delivery app. Success or failure in government could affect not just public opinion, but also public policy and even public health.

Although the tools eventually were made available to the turnaround team, it took months of effort, demonstrating small-scale successes, building trust between the coders and government staff, and recognizing that both sides had valuable perspectives and knowledge to offer.[3]

Beyond gathering varied individual perspectives to inform your understanding of context, you should also aim to diversify the types of information you collect. Additional sources of evidence include internal surveys (e.g., employee engagement), internal analyses on relevant topics, system reports, lessons learned from past changes, performance management systems, or industry reports.

View Context through a Readiness Lens

Perhaps the simplest way to analyze your context is to narrow your investigation to issues of "readiness." Readiness reflects the abilities and attitudes of the organization, and individual staff, related to the change implementation. Change readiness is linked with a variety of desirable organizational outcomes, such as change-supportive behaviors, satisfaction with the change, and the overall ability of the organization to dynamically adapt to changes.[4]

There are a variety of readiness frameworks offered by researchers. Here I have adapted that developed by Achilles Armenakis and colleagues, which suggests that readiness is related to a few key factors:[5]

- **The Need** — There is an identified problem to be solved or explicit consequences for not changing. There is a clear vision for the future, which is aligned with the organization's overall strategy.
- **Right Solution** — The innovation or solution that will be implemented is a good fit for the need, culture, and capacity of the organization.

- **Change Capability** — The organization, (and individuals within it), has the skills necessary to implement the change and use the innovation to create the desired outcomes.
- **Support** — The organization and its leaders clearly support and prioritize the change (with words, actions, and resourcing.)
- **Impact** — The impact the change will have on individuals and teams — both positive and negative — is understood.

Formal readiness assessment tools are commercially available; however, some research indicates that they may not be valid and reliable (i.e., they do not consistently measure what they say they measure).[6] Some of these assessments are also quite extensive and may not be appropriate for some organizations or smaller scale changes.

In lieu of a formal assessment tool, you can systematically investigate the planned change implementation in light of each readiness factor. This can be as straightforward as asking questions related to each factor, such as: What do we know about the need for this change? Are there any holes in our rationale that demand greater scrutiny? (See Figure 16 for examples.) In doing so, you can uncover potential issues you need to address or strengths that can support the change effort.

Readiness Factor	Relevant Information Sources	Responding to issues identified (Examples)
The Need Is the change necessary? How do we know? Are the vision and purpose of the change clear? Is the change aligned with the organization's strategy?	• Problem/Issue analysis • Internal/External reports • Stated goals or vision for change	• Additional problem analysis • Clarification of vision • Identification of key data to support communications • Reconsideration of need
Right Solution Is the proposed innovation a good fit for the need and the organization?	• Problem/Issue analysis • Decision analysis • Organizational Climate/Culture • Resources/Infrastructure • Available resources/existing infrastructure • Internal technical expertise	• Facilitate broader input into solution selection • Identify additional alternatives • Identify adaptations
Change Capability Are the organization and individual employees capable of implementing the change? Do necessary skills and capabilities exist or can they be learned?	• Type, scale, scope of intended change • Organizational history with change • Degree of concurrent change • Available resources/existing infrastructure • Leadership and individual readiness	• Consider piloting • Differentiate from failed efforts; highlight similarities with successes • Secure committed resources upfront or reconsider scale/scope of change • Training, coaching

Figure 16 Viewing Context through a Readiness Lens

Take a Deeper Look

For complex changes, you may want to use a more comprehensive approach to analyze your context. The process described in this section involves first sizing your change, followed by a review of the current environment. This two-step process can help you to understand the unique requirements of implementing the innovation in your current organizational context.

Let the change guide your implementation approach

Start by reflecting on the change you are implementing. This type of analysis will help you understand the complexity of the change and the level of skill and resources required to implement the innovation effectively. Gather information necessary to answer questions such as:

- **Scope** —What is the scope of the change? Who will be directly impacted by the change? A specific team, a department, the entire organization? Are those impacted co-located, or spread across a country, region, or globally? Are impacted groups similar or might you

need to adapt your approach to different sub-contexts?
- **Scale** — What is the scale of the change? Are you tweaking things or transforming them? How large an impact will it have? Will this change create winners and losers?
- **Uncertainty** —What is the degree of uncertainty about the innovation, adoption potential, or other aspects of the implementation? Is the innovation well defined? How much design, development, or customization of the innovation is required? How clear is the way forward? How certain are you about what's *not* changing?

You can use a simple scale such as small —medium — large to summarize your answer to each question. The scale will help you broadly understand the type of implementation approach that is required for the change. For instance, if the scope, scale, and uncertainty of the change are all large or high — all regions of a global organization are affected by what is currently an ill-defined, but high-impact innovation — your change approach will be quite different than if they are all low —one team is affected, the innovation is well defined with a moderate impact on current operations. You'll likely have a mix across the factors with some being lower and others higher.

See Figure 17 for examples of how you might tailor your approach based on your findings.

	Lower Complexity Change	Higher Complexity Change
Overall	• Moderate change skill • Less resources required • Lower visibility	• Advanced change skill • More resources required • Higher visibility
Scope	• Leverage existing infrastructure (team, governance, communications, reporting)	• Enhance existing or develop new infrastructure (team, governance, communications, reporting) • Broad outreach
Scale	• Modest support, training, coaching	• Extensive engagement • Comprehensive support, training, coaching
Uncertainty	• Feedback focused on satisfaction • Defined plans & measures	• Extensive engagement • Iterative planning • Short-term learning goals and long-term performance targets • Rapid feedback & learning

Figure 17 — Tailoring Your Approach to Your Context

Identify assets and challenges

Once you have a clear sense of the dimensions of the change, it's a good idea to gather specific information about the environment in which the change will be implemented. If the scope of the change is broad, it may be worthwhile to do the following step for major sub-contexts, such as specific regions, divisions, or teams. When conducting this aspect of the context analysis be on the look-out for a mismatch between the demands of your change (uncovered via the first step) and the current culture, capacity, and climate of the organization.

Some factors to investigate in this part of the analysis are listed below.

- **Clarity** — How clear is the rationale and vision for this change? Is it likely to resonate with people? What decision-making process was used to approve the change effort? What data exist to support the decision?
- **Priority** — What is the priority level of the current change? Do all impacted parties prioritize it similarly, or are there significant differences? Is this change competing with a large number of other changes for attention and resources?
- **History**— What is the organization's history of change?

Have past changes been positive experiences? Have there been recent failures, or have past changes been started and then abandoned?
- **Culture** — What aspects of the current culture or climate are significant? What are the current levels of trust, job satisfaction, or organizational commitment? Is the culture of the organization generally open to change or more conservative towards it? Is the organization formal, traditional, and hierarchical or informal, flexible, and innovative? How well do these factors align with the nature of the change and required approach?
- **Resources** — What infrastructure exists to support the effort? Are sufficient human, monetary, and physical resources available to support the implementation and ongoing use of the innovation?
- **Capability** — What is the current level of change capability in the organization? How much change experience do leaders have? How adaptable, resilient, and open to change are those who will be impacted? What relevant competencies do impacted staff hold related to the technical aspects of the innovation?

You can use a simple scale to summarize your evaluation of these factors, such as low — medium —high. Factors on the higher end of the scale represent assets, while those on the lower end reflect challenges you'll need to mitigate.

In addition to aspects of your internal environment, you may want to consider external factors that may impact your organization and influence the implementation, such as regulatory requirements, industry shifts, economic pressures, or the political climate.

Once you've identified key assets and challenges, work with your change team and relevant stakeholders to determine how you'll mitigate or leverage them. (See Figure 18 for some examples.) If challenges are significant, it's crucial that decision-makers are aware of their potential impact and proactive steps are taken to lessen them. Significant issues are unlikely to go away on their own!

	Low — Mitigate Challenges	High — Leverage Assets
Clarity	• Conduct additional problem analysis or vision definition	• Integrate into key messages • Use to guide decisions
Priority/ Resources	• Consider delay, sequencing, pilots	• Leverage to overcome select challenges • Set high performance standards
History with Change	• Differentiate from past (this is different because…)	• Adopt best practices from previous efforts • Highlight past successes
Culture	• Aim to meet unique stakeholder needs • Proactively address climate issues through change approach, as possible • Delay if climate is too challenged to support change	• Leverage trusted leaders and staff for key roles • Engage committed and open staff as change agents
Capability	• Hire external expertise • Offer leadership development and coaching (general or change specific) • Provide extensive support, training, and coaching • Set expectations for learning (slower pace)	• Use internal resources for key implementation roles • Provide targeted support; advanced training; train-the-trainers model; peer coaching

Figure 18 — Identifying Assets and Challenges

Still other options

While not as systematic as the approaches outlined previously, other options for identifying significant contextual factors include:

- **Integrating questions about context** into interviews, focus groups, or design sessions. You can identify themes from the input received to help you plan appropriate next steps.
- **Holding a premortem.** This technique involves asking a group to imagine themselves in a future state, where the implementation has been completed and has been an utter failure. You then ask them to "look back" from this imagined future to identify the major reasons for

the failure. While not all the issues identified will be contextual, you can expect many will be. You can then use the issues raised to inform your plans and approaches.

Regardless of the method you use, the key is to build awareness of the aspects of your context that are likely to be most impactful so that you can address them.

A note on timing

Because your choice of innovation may be impacted by context, you may need to identify contextual factors that are particularly relevant to that decision in the early stages of your effort. You can have a subsequent discussion on factors that should inform other aspects of your implementation approach once you have selected the innovation and assembled your implementation team.

Phases and Context

During the **Decide** phase, identify contextual factors that should inform your choice of innovation. These may include the size of your organization, available resources, the relevant skills of end users, and prevalent norms or culture. During the **Prepare** phase, consider contextual factors that should inform your training, communications, and engagement approaches. Usually, there is more than one way to do something; let your choice be informed by your context.

During the **Execution** phase, note additional assets or constraints that arise from your context. Adjust your approach as necessary during the **Improve** phase. Finally, during the **Maintain** phase, document the contextual factors that most influenced your implementation, including both those that worked for and those that worked against you. Such information can be a boon to future implementation efforts in your organization.

STARTER STEPS: Context

Context can influence many aspects of your implementation. Take time to identify the contextual factors that might have the biggest impact on your efforts. To do so:

1. **View context from diverse perspectives.** Regardless of the method used to gather input on your context, be sure you have a diverse group involved. This is particularly essential if you have limited experience working in your current context or for implementations that will have a broad impact.

2. **Tailor your approach to fit your change.** Consider the type, scope, scale and uncertainty level of the change you are implementing. Doing so will help you understand the degree of complexity of the change and other unique requirements that should inform your implementation approach.

3. **Identify challenges and assets in your current environment.** Use your understanding of change readiness to identify significant factors – such as levels of competence, resources, priorities, or history – that may affect how people perceive or use the innovation you are implementing. Know that these may differ across various groups impacted by the change. Design your implementation approach to address challenges and leverage assets proactively.

EXPERT TIPS

Think about context early on. Context should play into decision-making about the innovation you will implement and inform your plans for everything from training and coaching, to stakeholder engagement and performance measurement.

Assume you are missing something. We all have blind spots. Work from the assumption that you are missing something about your context and keep asking questions until you find out what it is.

Listen for repeated concerns. If you find people across the organization consistently list reasons for why something will not work for them, listen. They may be telling you something important about their culture or history that you should at least acknowledge, if not explicitly address, in your approach.

Notes

1. This case was adapted from Shanks, G., Parr, A., Hu, B., Corbitt, B., Thanasankit, T., & Seddon, P. (2000). Differences in critical success factors in ERP systems implementation in Australia and China: a cultural analysis. *ECIS 2000 Proceedings*, 53. Retrieved from https://aisel.aisnet.org/ecis2000/53
2. See, for example, Tomoaia-Cotisel, A., Scammon, D. L., Waitzman, N. J., Cronholm, P. F., Halladay, J. R., Driscoll, D. L., ... & Shih, S. C. (2013). Context matters: The experience of 14 research teams in systematically reporting contextual factors important for practice change. *The Annals of Family Medicine*, *11*(Suppl 1), S115-S123. doi:10.1370/afm.1549; Damschroder, L. J., Goodrich, D. E., Robinson, C. H., Fletcher, C. E., & Lowery, J. C. (2011). A systematic exploration of differences in contextual factors related to implementing the MOVE! weight management program in VA: A mixed methods study. *BMC Health Services Research*, *11*(1), 248. Retrieved from http://www.biomedcentral.com/1472-6963/11/248; or Hamilton, A. B., Mittman, B. S., Eccles, A. M., Hutchinson, C. S., & Wyatt, G. E. (2015). Conceptualizing and measuring external context in implementation science: Studying the impacts of regulatory, fiscal, technological and social change. *Implementation Science*, *10*. doi:10.1186/1748-5908-10-S1-A72
3. This example was adapted from Levy, S. (2014, June 5). Why the new Obamacare website is going to work this time. *Wired*. Retrieved from https://www.wired.com/2014/06/healthcare-gov-revamp/; Meyer, R. (2015, July 9). The secret startup that saved the worst website in America. *The Atlantic*. Retrieved from https://www.theatlantic.com/technology/archive/2015/07/the-secret-startup-saved-healthcare-gov-the-worst-website-in-america/397784/; and Roose, K. (2014, June 6). What Silicon Valley doesn't get about government tech. *New York*. Retrieved from http://nymag.com/daily/intelligencer/2014/06/what-silicon-valley-doesnt-get-about-gov-tech.html
4. See, for example, Santhidran, S., Chandran, V. G. R., & Borromeo, J. (2013). Enabling organizational change – leadership, commitment to change and the mediating role of change readiness. *Journal of Business Economics and Management*, *14*(2), 348-363. doi: 10.3846/16111699.2011.642083 or Holt, D. T., Armenakis, A. A., Feild, H. S., & Harris, S. G. (2016). Readiness for Organizational Change: The Systematic Development of a Scale. *The Journal of Applied Behavioral Science*, *43*(2), 232-255. doi: 10.1177/0021886306295295

5. Adaptations largely relate to using more accessible terminology (i.e., using "need" versus "discrepancy"). For a discussion of the original framework, see Armenakis, A. A., Harris, S. G., & Mossholder, K. W. (2016). Creating Readiness for Organizational Change. *Human Relations*, 46(6), 681-703. doi: 10.1177/001872679304600601
6. See, for example, Weiner, B. J., Amick, H., & Lee, S. Y. (2008). Conceptualization and measurement of organizational readiness for change: a review of the literature in health services research and other fields. *Medical Care Research Review*, 65(4), 379-436. doi: 10.1177/1077558708317802

A FINAL NOTE...

MAKE THE MOST OF IT

One of the reasons I enjoy implementation is that it is full of promise. When we help to create and execute change in an organization, we have a unique chance to transform an idea into a reality, and ultimately, results.

Throughout this book, I have provided you with methods and tools you can use to help your organization turn its great ideas into great achievements. As you begin to put these into practice, I encourage you not to lose sight of the sense of possibility inherent in all change implementations.

Make the most of this opportunity

Implementation offers an excellent chance for on-the-job professional development. Take advantage of this opportunity by assessing your skills and crafting a simple development plan for yourself before things get too hectic. (Encourage your team members to do so as well.)

You can use the implementation framework to evaluate your strengths and growth areas. What skills are most familiar and recognizable to you as strengths? Which areas may be new and require you to experiment or undertake additional study and practice? To fill out the picture, consider getting informal input from colleagues, supervisors, and others.

Write down a few professional development goals that you aim to accomplish during the implementation — the more specific, the better. Take it a step further and share your goals with your team or supervisor; it's a great way to ensure these goals don't fall by the wayside.

If you feel a new assignment may be particularly challenging, consider working with a coach or signing up for relevant training courses to keep you ahead of the curve.

Finally, remember you probably shouldn't aim to be the best in everything. Implementation is a team effort. It's just as important to learn how to bring out the best in others.

Take care of yourself

Change implementation often requires long hours for an extended period. Burnout is a real risk. To ensure you can give your best to the project and your team, take care of yourself. Even when you are busy, prioritize essential aspects of self-care, such as sleep, exercise, and taking real breaks. You'll not only feel better, but you'll probably also perform better.

Additionally, some research indicates there may be a link between humor, motivation, and persistence.[1] A little levity may create a mental break or "psychological vacation" from the pressing concerns of work. Rather than being detrimental to your efforts, creating a sense of play and taking time for amusement may help you and your team to persevere through challenging times. So, go ahead and smile! It's encouraged!

Keep learning

Many of the ideas that informed this book were developed collaboratively, through the exchange of views and experiences with other practitioners. In my opinion, time spent learning with others is time well spent. Therefore, if you have the opportunity,

I encourage you to join a relevant community of practice in your organization or local community. If none exist, consider creating an informal discussion group.

I also hope we can continue our learning together. To that end, I invite you to visit my blog at wendyhirsch.com, which I continually update with new ideas, case studies, tools, and research related to change implementation and team development.

Whatever the method, I encourage you to keep experimenting and stretching yourself. Because, as Winston Churchill so aptly observed, "To improve is to change, so to be perfect is to have changed often."

Notes

1. See Cheng, D., & Wang, L. (2015). Examining the energizing effects of humor: The influence of humor on persistence behavior. *Journal of Business and Psychology, 30*(4), 759-772. https://doi.org/10.1007/s10869-014-9396-z

IMPLEMENTATION CHECKLIST

This checklist is an example of how you can apply learning from this book to your next implementation. It is not exhaustive; view it as a first draft and add elements based on your experience and context. (A printable version of this checklist is available at wendyhirsch.com.)

DECIDE PHASE

The purpose, vision and desired outcomes of the implementation are defined and approved by relevant decision-makers.

Innovation options are assessed for fit to our needs, desired outcomes, available resources, and capabilities. An option is selected.

- Critical contextual factors are identified.
- Significant adaptations are identified.
- A decision has been made on whether or not a pilot will be conducted.

High-level infrastructure and resourcing requirements are estimated and agreed to.

- Not to exceed budget is set.
- Staffing requirements (contractors/FTEs) are estimated.
- The executive sponsor is identified.
- The implementation lead is identified.

- The maximum time frame for the implementation is agreed to.
- Critical infrastructure requirements are identified.

PREPARE PHASE

The implementation team is assembled.

- All key roles are filled.
- Norms and team processes are developed.

The innovation is documented.

- Relevant stakeholders are engaged in design or input sessions.
- Core components/effectiveness factors are clear.
- Adaptations are explicit.
- Areas open to modification by end users are highlighted.

The implementation plan is developed.

- A master task list or work breakdown structure is created and aligned with a schedule and budget. Tasks are assigned to key roles.
- The governance framework is clarified, governance body members appointed, and a schedule of meetings developed.
- The measurement system is developed, including clarification of what will be measured, how it will be measured, how related work will be organized, and how findings will be used.
- The communication and engagement plan is in place. Key stakeholders and end user groups are identified.
- Training and coaching approaches are developed — learning objectives are identified, training materials developed, and training dates scheduled; coaching par-

ticipants are selected and coaches secured.

EXECUTE PHASE

The implementation plan is executed.

- Training is provided as scheduled.
- Coaching and support sessions are executed.
- Data collection and analysis are undertaken as planned.
- Team debriefs are held to identify learning and log potential adaptations to be made in future phases.
- Two-way communication with end users and stakeholders is ongoing. Progress information is provided on a regular basis.

The implementation team actively assists end users in adoption, providing real-time support and troubleshooting issues as they arise.

Progress is regularly reviewed by the implementation team, sponsor, and governance body.

IMPROVE PHASE

Improvements are recommended, prioritized, and approved by relevant groups, per the governance framework.

- Quantitative and qualitative progress data are analyzed and potential improvements identified. Implications, including resource requirements, are estimated.
- Improvements are prioritized and approved by relevant decision-makers.
- End users and key stakeholders are informed of improvements that will be made in future execution cycles.

Plans are updated to incorporate improvements and other necessary adjustments to guide additional Execute phases.

(At the conclusion of this phase, loop back to previous phases as necessary. If you haven't done so already, be sure to schedule a time to celebrate successes with team members and end users!)

MAINTAIN PHASE

The transition plan and schedule are finalized.

- The owner or manager who will oversee the innovation under normal operations is confirmed.
- Required resources for ongoing maintenance are approved.
- Timeframe and scope of transition activities are agreed to by all parties.

Key learnings are identified and documented.

- Debriefs are held with the implementation team and key stakeholders.
- Major findings from the measurement program are summarized and communicated.

Key documents, including measurement data, plans, and training materials, are archived or transitioned to support organizational learning.

The transition to the maintenance team is complete.

IMPLEMENTATION FRAMEWORK

A printable version of the implementation framework is available at wendyhirsch.com.

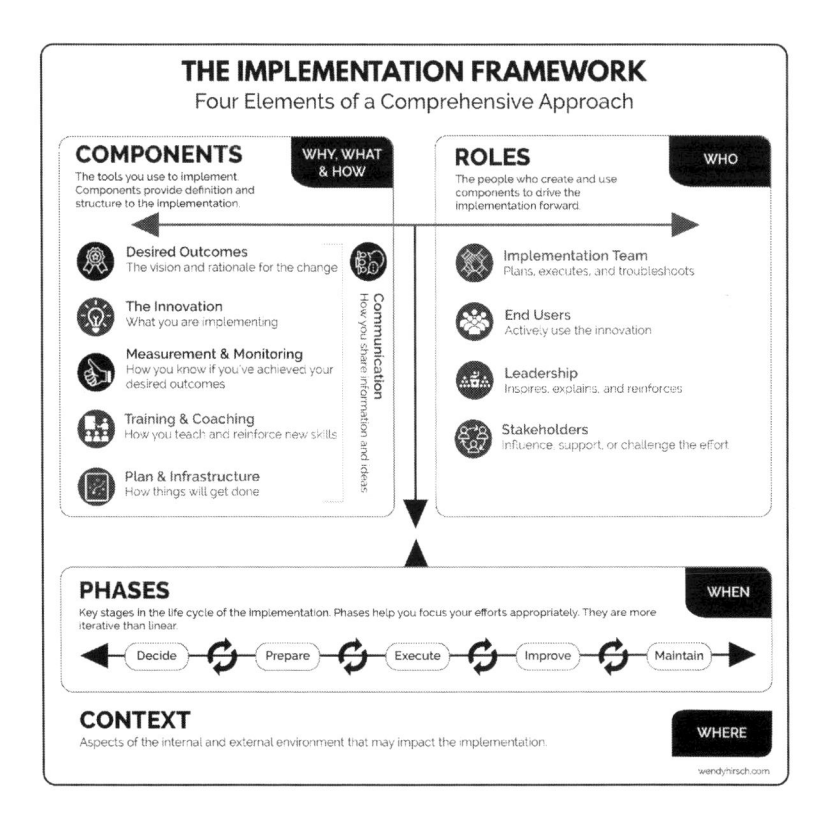

THE IMPLEMENTATION FRAMEWORK
Four Elements of a Comprehensive Approach

COMPONENTS — WHY, WHAT & HOW
The tools you use to implement. Components provide definition and structure to the implementation.

- **Desired Outcomes** — The vision and rationale for the change
- **The Innovation** — What you are implementing
- **Measurement & Monitoring** — How you know if you've achieved your desired outcomes
- **Training & Coaching** — How you teach and reinforce new skills
- **Plan & Infrastructure** — How things will get done

Communication — How you share information and ideas

ROLES — WHO
The people who create and use components to drive the implementation forward.

- **Implementation Team** — Plans, executes, and troubleshoots
- **End Users** — Actively use the innovation
- **Leadership** — Inspires, explains, and reinforces
- **Stakeholders** — Influence, support, or challenge the effort

PHASES — WHEN
Key stages in the life cycle of the implementation. Phases help you focus your efforts appropriately. They are more iterative than linear.

Decide → Prepare → Execute → Improve → Maintain

CONTEXT — WHERE
Aspects of the internal and external environment that may impact the implementation.

wendyhirsch.com

LIST OF FIGURES

Part II: What

Figure 1: The Implementation Framework — p. 41

Figure 2: Components — p. 42

Figure 3: Roles — p. 44

Figure 4: Phases — p. 45

Part III: When

Figure 5: Phases — p. 49

Part IV: How

Figure 6: Measurement Framework — p. 91

Figure 7: Monitoring and Measurement Plan — p. 96

Figure 8: Plan Examples — p. 121

Figure 9: Governance Framework — p. 123

Part V: Who

Figure 10: General Team Structure — p. 148

Figure 11: ERP Structure — p. 151

Figure 12: Process Improvement Structure — p. 152

Figure 13: System-wide Strategy Structure — p. 153

Figure 14: The Role of the Sponsor — p. 167

Figure 15: Stakeholders Matrix — p. 193

Part VI: Where

Figure 16: Viewing Context through a Readiness Lens — p. 210

Figure 17: Tailoring Your Approach to Your Context — p. 212

Figure 18: Responding to Challenges and Assets — p. 214

BIBLIOGRAPHY

(2018). Abebooks closes accounts and withdraws from several markets. Retrieved from https://ilab.org/articles/abebooks-closes-accounts-and-withdraws-several-markets

Acasus. (2014, February 12). The Chief Minister's Roadmap. [Blog post]. Retrieved from https://www.acasus.com/insights/2017/8/11/the-chief-ministers-roadmap

Ackermann, F., & Eden, C. (2011). Strategic management of stakeholders: Theory and practice. *Long range planning, 44*(3), 179-196. doi:10.1016/j.lrp.2010.08.001

Allen, J., Jimmieson, N. L., Bordia, P., & Irmer, B. E. (2007). Uncertainty during Organizational Change: Managing Perceptions through Communication. *Journal of Change Management, 7*(2), 187-210. doi:10.1080/14697010701563379

Armenakis, A. A., & Harris, S. G. (2009). Reflections: Our journey in organizational change research and practice. *Journal of Change Management, 9*(2), 127-142. doi:10.1080/14697010902879079

Armenakis, A. A., Harris, S. G., & Mossholder, K. W. (2016). Creating Readiness for Organizational Change. *Human Relations, 46*(6), 681-703. doi:10.1177/001872679304600601

Armitage, C. J., & Conner, M. (2001). Efficacy of the theory of planned behaviour: A meta-analytic review. *British journal of social psychology, 40*(4), 471-499. Retrieved from doi: 10.1348/014466601164939

Balogun, J. (2003). From Blaming the Middle to Harnessing its Potential: Creating Change Intermediaries. *British Journal of Management*, *14*(1), 69-83. doi:10.1111/1467-8551.00266

Barends, E., Janssen, B., & Velghe, C. (2016). Technical report: Rapid evidence assessment of the research literature on the effect of goal setting on workplace performance (pp.1-19). London: Chartered Institute of Personnel and Development (CIPD). Retrieved from https://www.cipd.co.uk/Images/rapid-evidence-assessment-of-the-research-literature-on-the-effect-of-goal-setting-on-workplace-performance_tcm18-16903.pdf

Battilana, J., Gilmartin, M., Sengul, M., Pache, A. C., & Alexander, J. A. (2010). Leadership competencies for implementing planned organizational change. *The Leadership Quarterly*, *21*(3), 422-438. doi:10.1016/j.leaqua.2010.03.007

Bauer, M. S., Damschroder, L., Hagedorn, H., Smith, J., & Kilbourne, A. M. (2015). An introduction to implementation science for the non-specialist. *BMC Psychology*, *3*(1), 32. doi:10.1186/s40359-015-0089-9

Beierle, T. C. (2002). The quality of stakeholder-based decisions. *Risk analysis*, *22*(4), 739-749. doi:10.1111/0272-4332.00065

Bertram, R. M., Blase, K. A., & Fixsen, D. L. (2015). Improving programs and outcomes: Implementation frameworks and organization change. *Research on Social Work Practice*, *25*, 477-487. doi:10.1177/1049731514537687

Bohrnstedt, G. W., & Stecher, B. M. (2002). What we have learned about class size reduction in California. Sacramento, CA: California Department of Education. Retrieved from http://www.classize.org/techreport/CSRYear4_final.pdf

Bouckenooghe, D. (2012). The role of organizational politics, contextual resources, and formal communication on change recipients' commitment to change: A multilevel study. *European Journal of Work and Organizational Psychology, 21*(4), 575-602. doi:10.1080/1359432X.2011.591573

Bowen, F., Newenham-Kahindi, A., & Herremans, I. (2010). When suits meet roots: The antecedents and consequences of community engagement strategy. *Journal of Business Ethics, 95*(2), 297-318. doi:10.1007/s10551-009-0360-1

Bradley, D. K. F., & Griffin, M. (2016). The Well Organised Working Environment: A mixed methods study. *International Journal of Nursing Studies, 55*, 26-38. Retrieved from http://repository.essex.ac.uk/id/eprint/15543

Bryson, J. M. (2004). What to do when stakeholders matter: Stakeholder identification and analysis techniques. *Public Management Review, 6*(1), 21-53. doi:10.1080/14719030410001675722

Burnes, B. (2004). Kurt Lewin and the planned approach to change: A re-appraisal. *Journal of Management Studies, 41*(6), 977-1002. doi: 10.1111/j.1467-6486.2004.00463.x

Cheng, D., & Wang, L. (2015). Examining the energizing effects of humor: The influence of humor on persistence behavior. *Journal of Business and Psychology, 30*(4), 759-772. https://doi.org/10.1007/s10869-014-9396-z

Choo, A. S. (2014). Defining problems fast and slow: The u-shaped effect of problem definition time on project duration. *Production and Operations Management, 23*(8), 1462-1479. doi: 10.1111/poms.12219

Coca-Cola fans share their stories. (2012, January 1). Retrieved from http://www.coca-colacompany.com/stories/coca-cola-stories-new-coke

Damschroder, L. J., Goodrich, D. E., Robinson, C. H., Fletcher, C. E., & Lowery, J. C. (2011). A systematic exploration of differences in contextual factors related to implementing the MOVE! weight management program in VA: A mixed methods study. *BMC Health Services Research, 11*(1), 248. Retrieved from http://www.biomedcentral.com/1472-6963/11/248

DeShong, T. (2017, October 13). LEAD by example. *The Yale Herald.* Retrieved from https://yaleherald.com/lead-by-example-8645e6251531

Detrich, R. (2013). Innovation, implementation science, and data-based decision making: Components of successful reform. In S. R. M. Murphy, & J. Twyman (Ed.), *Handbook on innovations in learning* (pp. 31-48). Retrieved from http://www.centeril.org/

Domitrovich, C. E., Bradshaw, C. P., Poduska, J. M., Hoagwood, K., Buckley, J. A., Olin, S. & Ialongo, N. S. (2008). Maximizing the implementation quality of evidence-based preventive interventions in schools: A conceptual framework. *Advances in School Mental Health Promotion, 1*(3), 6-28. Retrieved from https://www.ncbi.nlm.nih.gov/pmc/articles/PMC4865398/

Durlak, J. (2013). The importance of quality implementation for research, practice, and policy. *ASPE Research Brief.* U.S. Department of Health and Human Services. Retrieved from https://aspe.hhs.gov/report/importance-quality-implementation-research-practice-and-policy

Durlak, J. A., DuPre, E. P. (2008). Implementation matters: A review of research on the influence of implementation on program outcomes and the factors affecting implementation. *American Journal of Community Psychology, 41*(3-4), 327-350. doi: 10.1007/s10464-008-9165-0

Echt, L., & Weyrauch, V. (2017). Going beyond 'context matters': A lens to bridge knowledge and policy. Retrieved from https://i2insights.org/2017/04/25/how-context-matters/

Erwin, D. G., & Garman, A. N. (2010). Resistance to organizational change: Linking research and practice. *Leadership & Organization Development Journal, 31*(1), 39-56. doi:10.1108/01437731011010371

Fagan, A. A., Hanson, K., Hawkins, J. D., & Arthur, M. W. (2008). Bridging science to practice: Achieving prevention program implementation fidelity in the Community Youth Development Study. *American Journal of Community Psychology, 41*(3-4), 235-249. doi:10.1007/s10464-008-9176-x

Flood, A. (2018). Booksellers unite in protest as Amazon's AbeBooks withdraws from several countries. Retrieved from Retrieved from https://www.theguardian.com/books/2018/nov/06/booksellers-protest-amazon-abebooks-withdraw-russia-south-korea

Ford, J. D., & Ford, L. W. (2012). The leadership of organization change: A view from recent empirical evidence. In Research in Organizational Change and Development (pp. 1-36). Emerald Group Publishing Limited. doi:10.1108/S0897-3016(2012)0000020004

Gary, M. S., Yang, M. M., Yetton, P. W., & Sterman, J. D. (2017). Stretch goals and the distribution of organizational performance. *Organization Science. 28*(3), 395-410. doi:10.1287/orsc.2017.1131

Gefen, D., & Ridings, C. (2002). Implementation team responsiveness and user evaluation of customer relationship management: A quasi-experimental design study of social exchange theory. *Journal of Management Information Systems, 19*(1), 47-69. doi:10.1080/07421222.2002.11045717

Gold, J. (2016, January 19). Delivering development: Lessons from DFID's implementation units. [Blog post]. Retrieved from https://www.instituteforgovernment.org.uk/blog/delivering-development-lessons-dfid%E2%80%99s-implementation-units

Greenhalgh, T., Robert, G., Macfarlane, F., Bate, P., & Kyriakidou, O. (2004). Diffusion of innovations in service organizations: Systematic review and recommendations. *Milbank Quarterly, 82*(4), 581-629. doi:10.1111/j.0887-378X.2004.00325.x

Guldbrandsson, K. (2008). From news to everyday use: The difficult art of implementation. *Statens Folkhälsoinstitut, Rapport R* (9). Retrieved from http://www.who.int/management/district/services/FromNewstoEverydayUse.pdf

Hackman, J. R., & Edmondson, A. C. (2008). Groups as agents of change. In T. Cummings (Ed.), *Handbook of organization development* (pp. 167-186). Thousand Oaks, CA: Sage.

Hackman, J. R., & Wageman, R. (2004). When and how team leaders matter. *Research in Organizational Behavior, 26,* 37-74. doi: 10.1016/S0191-3085(04)26002-6

Hamilton, A. B., Mittman, B. S., Eccles, A. M., Hutchinson, C. S., & Wyatt, G. E. (2015). Conceptualizing and measuring external context in implementation science: Studying the impacts of regulatory, fiscal, technological and social change. *Implementation Science, 10.* doi:10.1186/1748-5908-10-S1-A72

Harkin, B., Webb, T. L., Chang, B. P., Prestwich, A., Conner, M., Kellar, I., & Sheeran, P. (2016). Does monitoring goal progress promote goal attainment? A meta-analysis of the experimental evidence. *Psychological Bulletin, 142*(2), 198-229. doi:10.1037/bul0000025

Hartge, T., Callahan, T., & King, C. (2018). Leaders' Behaviors During Radical Change Processes: Subordinates' Perceptions of How Well Leader Behaviors Communicate Change. *International Journal of Business Communication, 56*(1), 100-121. doi:10.1177/2329488415605061

Heifetz, R. A., & Laurie, D. L. (1997). The work of leadership. *Harvard Business Review, 75*(1), 124-134. Retrieved from https://hbr.org/2001/12/the-work-of-leadership

Heifetz, R. A., & Linsky, M. (2002). *Leadership on the line: Staying alive through the dangers of leading.* Boston: Harvard Business School Press.

Heyden, M. L. M., Fourné, S. P. L., Koene, B. A. S., Werkman, R., & Ansari, S. S. (2017). Rethinking 'Top-Down' and 'Bottom-Up' Roles of Top and Middle Managers in Organizational Change: Implications for Employee Support. *Journal of Management Studies, 54*(7), 961-985. doi:10.1111/joms.12258

Higgins, M. C., Weiner, J., & Young, L. (2012). Implementation teams: A new lever for organizational change. *Journal of Organizational Behavior, 33*(3), 366-388. doi:10.1002/job.1773

Hirsch, W. (2017, April 21). Want your team to make better decisions? Be sure they do this. [Blog post]. Retrieved from http://wendyhirsch.com/blog/team-better-decision-process

Holten, A. L., & Brenner, S. O. (2015). Leadership style and the process of organizational change. *Leadership & Organization Development Journal, 36*(1), 2-16. doi:10.1108/LODJ-11-2012-0155

Infrastructure. (2017) In *Oxford English dictionary online.* (2nd ed). Retrieved from https://en.oxforddictionaries.com/definition/infrastructure

Kanter, R. M. (1982). Dilemmas of managing participation. *Organizational Dynamics, 11*(1), 5-27. doi:10.1016/0090-2616(82)90039-0

Kelly, J. A., Somlai, A. M., DiFranceisco, W. J., Otto-Salaj, L. L., McAuliffe, T. L., Hackl, K. L., ... & Rompa, D. (2000). Bridging the gap between the science and service of HIV prevention: transferring effective research-based HIV prevention interventions to community AIDS service providers. *American Journal of Public Health, 90*(7), 1082. Retrieved from https://www.ncbi.nlm.nih.gov/pmc/articles/PMC1446305/

Klein, G. (2007). Performing a project premortem. *Harvard Business Review, 85*(9), 18-19. Retrieved from https://hbr.org/2007/09/performing-a-project-premortem

Kotter, J. P. (2009). Leading change: Why transformation efforts fail. *Harvard Business Review, 73*(2). Retrieved from https://hbr.org/2007/01/leading-change-why-transformation-efforts-fail

Lam, S. S. K., & Schaubroeck, J. (2000). A field experiment testing frontline opinion leaders as change agents. *Journal of Applied Psychology, 85*(6), 987. doi:10.1037/0021-9010.85.6.987

Lee, S. J., Altschul, I., & Mowbray, C. T. (2008). Using planned adaptation to implement evidence-based programs with new populations. *American Journal of Community Psychology, 41*(3-4), 290-303. doi:10.1007/s10464-008-9160-5

Levy, S. (2014). Why the new Obamacare website is going to work this time. *Wired.* Retrieved from https://www.wired.com/2014/06/healthcare-gov-revamp/

Lindland, E., Fond, M., Haydon, A., Volmert, A., & Kendall-Taylor, N. (2015). *"Just Do It": Communicating implementation science and practice. A FrameWorks Strategic Report.* Washington, DC: FrameWorks Institute. Retrieved from https://www.frameworksinstitute.org/evidence-and-implementation1.html

Locke, E. A., & Latham, G. P. (2002). Building a practically useful theory of goal setting and task motivation: A 35-year odyssey. *American Psychologist, 57*(9), 705-717. doi:10.1037/0003-066X.57.9.705

Maor, D., & Reich, A. (2017). The people power of transformations. Retrieved from https://www.mckinsey.com/business-functions/organization/our-insights/the-people-power-of-transformations

Marinova, S. V., Peng, C., Lorinkova, N., Van Dyne, L., & Chiaburu, D. (2015). Change-oriented behavior: A meta-analysis of individual and job design predictors. *Journal of Vocational Behavior, 88*, 104-120. doi:10.1016/j.jvb.2015.02.006

Mayer, R. C., Davis, J. H., & Schoorman, F. D. (1995). An integrative model of organizational trust. *Academy of Management Review, 20*(3), 709-734. doi:10.5465/AMR.1995.9508080335

Meyer, R. (2015). The secret startup that saved the worst website in America. *The Atlantic.* Retrieved from www.theatlantic.com/technology/archive/2015/07/the-secret-startup-saved-healthcare-gov-the-worst-website-in-america/397784/

Meyers, D. C., Durlak, J.A., & Wandersman, A. (2012). The quality implementation framework: A synthesis of critical steps in the implementation process. *American Journal of Community Psychology, 50*(3-4), 462-480. doi:10.1007/s10464-012-9522-x

Miller, K., & Monge, P. (1985). Social information and employee anxiety about organizational change. *Human Communication Research, 11*(3), 365-386. doi:10.1111/j.1468-2958.1985.tb00052.x

Miller, S. (1997). Implementing strategic decisions: Four key success factors. *Organization Studies, 18*(4), 557-602. doi:10.1177/017084069701800402

Noble, C. H. (1999). The eclectic roots of strategy implementation research. *Journal of Business Research, 45*(2), 119-134. doi:10.1016/S0148-2963(97)00231-2

Northridge, M. E., & Metcalf, S. S. (2016). Enhancing implementation science by applying best principles of systems science. *Health Research Policy and Systems, 14*(1), 74. doi:10.1186/s12961-016-0146-8

Nutt, P. C. (1986). Tactics of implementation. *Academy of Management Journal, 29*(2), 230-261. doi:10.2307/256187

Oreg, S., Vakola, M., & Armenakis, A. (2011). Change recipients' reactions to organizational change: A 60-year review of quantitative studies. *The Journal of Applied Behavioral Science, 47*(4), 461-524. doi:10.1177/0021886310396550

Pasmore, W. A., & Fagans, M. R. (1992). Participation, individual development, and organizational change: A review and synthesis. *Journal of Management, 18*(2), 375-397. doi:10.1177/014920639201800208

Peachman, R. R. (2017, May 24). Put your baby in a box? Experts advise caution. *The New York Times*. Retrieved from https://nyti.ms/2qWutnY

Rafferty, A. E., Jimmieson, N. L., & Armenakis, A. A. (2013). Change readiness: A multilevel review. *Journal of Management, 39*(1), 110-135. doi:10.1177/0149206312457417

Ranganath, B. G. (2010). Coverage survey for assessing mass drug administration against lymphatic filariasis in Gulbarga district, Karnataka, India. *Journal of Vector Borne Diseases, 47*(1), 61- 64. Retrieved from https://www.ncbi.nlm.nih.gov/pubmed/20231778

Reinke, W. M., Stormont, M., Herman, K. C., & Newcomer, L. (2014). Using coaching to support teacher implementation of classroom-based interventions. *Journal of Behavioral Education, 23*(1), 150-167. doi:10.1007/s10864-013-9186-0

Repenning, N., Keifer, D., & Astor, T. (2017). The most underrated skill in management. *MIT Sloan Management Review, 58*(3), 39. Retrieved from http://sloanreview.mit.edu/article/the-most-underrated-skill-in-management/[/footnote]

Rhim, L. M., Kowal, J. M., Hassel, B. C., & Hassel, E. A. (2007). *School turnarounds: A review of the cross-sector evidence on dramatic organizational improvement*. Lincoln, IL: Center on Innovation and Improvement. Retrieved from http://www.centerii.org/survey/downloads/Turnarounds-Color.pdf

Roose, K. (2014). What Silicon Valley doesn't get about government tech. *New York*. Retrieved from http://nymag.com/daily/intelligencer/2014/06/what-silicon-valley-doesnt-get-about-gov-tech.html

Salas, E., Shuffler, M. L., Thayer, A. L., Bedwell, W. L., & Lazzara, E. H. (2015). Understanding and improving teamwork in organizations: A scientifically based practical guide. *Human Resource Management, 54*(4), 599-622. doi: 10.1002/hrm.21628

Salas, E., Tannenbaum, S. I., Kraiger, K., & Smith-Jentsch, K. A. (2012). The science of training and development in organizations: What matters in practice. *Psychological Science in the Public Interest,* 13(2), 74-101. doi:10.1177/1529100612436661.

Santhidran, S., Chandran, V. G. R., & Borromeo, J. (2013). Enabling organizational change – leadership, commitment to change and the mediating role of change readiness. *Journal of Business Economics and Management, 14*(2), 348-363. doi:10.3846/16111699.2011.642083

Schaubroeck, J., May, D. R., & Brown, F. W. (1994). Procedural justice explanations and employee reactions to economic hardship: A field experiment. *Journal of Applied Psychology, 79*(3), 455. doi: 10.1037/0021-9010.79

Schneider, H., English, R., Tabana, H., Padayachee, T., & Orgill, M. (2014). Whole-system change: Case study of factors facilitating early implementation of a primary health care reform in a South African province. *BMC Health Services Research, 14*(1). 609. doi:10.1186/s12913-014-0609-y

Schweiger, D. M., & Denisi, A. S. (1991). Communication with employees following a merger: A longitudinal field experiment. *Academy of Management Journal, 34*(1), 110-135. doi:10.5465/256304

Scott, M. (2017, October 03). Why Spectrum Health is teaching doctors about nutrition, cooking. Retrieved from http://www.mlive.com/news/grand-rapids/index.ssf/2017/10/how_spectrum_health_teaching_r.html

Serrador, P., & Turner, R. (2015).What is enough planning? Results from a global quantitative study. *IEEE Transactions on Engineering Management,* 62(4), 462-474. doi:10.1109/TEM.2015.2448059

Shanks, G., Parr, A., Hu, B., Corbitt, B., Thanasankit, T., & Seddon, P. (2000). Differences in critical success factors in ERP systems implementation in Australia and China: A cultural analysis. *ECIS 2000 Proceedings, 53*. Retrieved from https://aisel.aisnet.org/ecis2000/53

Simons, T., Leroy, H., Collewaert, V., & Masschelein, S. (2015). How Leader Alignment of Words and Deeds Affects Followers: A Meta-analysis of Behavioral Integrity Research. *Journal of Business Ethics, 132*(4), 831-844. doi:10.1007/s10551-014-2332-3

Sitkin, S. B., See, K. E., Miller, C. C., Lawless, M. W., & Carton, A. M. (2011). The paradox of stretch goals: Organizations in pursuit of the seemingly impossible. *Academy of Management Review, 36*(3), 544-566. doi:10.5465/amr.2008.0038

Sloan, P. (2009). Redefining stakeholder engagement: From control to collaboration. *Journal of Corporate Citizenship, 36*, 25-40. Retrieved from http://www.ingentaconnect.com/content/glbj/jcc/2009/00002009/00000036/art00005?crawler=true

Stakeholder matrix — key matrices for stakeholder analysis. (n.d.). Retrieved from https://www.stakeholdermap.com/stakeholder-matrix.html#dragan

Stecher, B. M. & Bohrnstedt, G. W. (Eds.). (2002). Class size reduction in California: Findings from 1999–00 and 2000–01. Sacramento, CA: California Department of Education. Retrieved from https://www.classsizematters.org/wp-content/uploads/2012/11/year3_technicalreport.pdf

Stouten, J., Rousseau, D., & De Cremer, D. (2018). Successful organizational change: Integrating the management practice and scholarly literatures. *Academy of Management Annals, 12*(2), 752-788. Retrieved from doi:10.5465/annals.2016.0095

Sutherland, S., & Palma, J. (2017, September 22). Preventing acute kidney injury: NINJA report. [Webinar]. Retrieved from http://www.himss.org/library/lucile-packard-children-s-hospital-stanford-and-stanford-children-s-health-davies-enterprise-award

Tannenbaum, S. I., & Cerasoli, C. P. (2013). Do team and individual debriefs enhance performance? A meta-analysis. *Human Factors, 55*(1), 231-245. doi:10.1177/0018720812448394

Taylor, A. & Kahn, J. (1997). How Toyota defies gravity. *Fortune, 136*(11), 100-106. Retrieved from http://archive.fortune.com/magazines/fortune/fortune_archive/

ten Have, S., ten Have, W., Huijsmans, A. B., & Otto, M. (2016). Reconsidering change management: Applying evidence-based insights in change management practice. Routledge.

The real story of New Coke. (2012, November 14). Retrieved from http://www.coca-colacompany.com/stories/coke-lore-new-coke

Thorp, F. (2013, October 31). Only 6 able to sign up on healthcare.gov's first day, documents show. Retrieved from https://www.nbcnews.com/news/other/only-6-able-sign-healthcare-govs-first-day-documents-show-f8C11509571

Tomoaia-Cotisel, A., Scammon, D. L., Waitzman, N. J., Cronholm, P. F., Halladay, J. R., Driscoll, D. L., & Shih, S. C. (2013). Context matters: The experience of 14 research teams in systematically reporting contextual factors important for practice change. *The Annals of Family Medicine, 11*(Suppl 1), S115-S123. doi:10.1370/afm.1549

Tornatzky, L. G., & Klein, K. J. (1982). Innovation characteristics and innovation adoption-implementation: A meta-analysis of findings. *IEEE Transactions on Engineering Management, EM-29*(1), 28-43. doi:10.1109/TEM.1982.6447463

U.S. Department of Health and Human Services. Office of the Inspector General. (2016). *Healthcare.gov: CMS management of the Federal Mar-*

ketplace. A case study. (DHHS Publication No. OEI-06-14-00350). Washington, DC: U.S. Government Printing Office. Retrieved from https://oig.hhs.gov/oei/reports/oei-06-14-00350.pdf

Van Dam, K., Oreg, S., & Schyns, B. (2008). Daily work contexts and resistance to organisational change: The role of leader–member exchange, development climate, and change process characteristics. *Applied Psychology, 57*(2), 313-334. doi:10.1111/j.1464-0597.2007.00311x

Wandersman, A., Duffy, J., Flaspohler, P., Noonan, R., Lubell, K., Stillman, L., & Saul, J. (2008). Bridging the gap between prevention research and practice: The interactive systems framework for dissemination and implementation. *American Journal of Community Psychology, 41*(3-4), 171-181. doi:10.1007/s10464-008-9174-z

Wandersman, A., Chien, V. H., & Katz, J. (2012). Toward an evidence-based system for innovation support for implementing innovations with quality: Tools, training, technical assistance, and quality assurance/quality improvement. *American Journal of Community Psychology, 50*(3-4), 445-459. doi:10.1007/s10464-012-9509-7

Weiner, B. J., Amick, H., & Lee, S. Y. (2008). Conceptualization and measurement of organizational readiness for change: a review of the literature in health services research and other fields. *Medical Care Research Review, 65*(4), 379-436. doi:10.1177/1077558708317802

Were, N., & Lin, H. (2017). The long road to branchless banking 2017. Retrieved from https://www.finca.org/about-finca/finca-publications/case-studies/long-road-branchless-banking/

Wilson, E. J., & Sherrell, D. L. (1993). Source effects in communication and persuasion research: A meta-analysis of effect size. *Journal of the Academy of Marketing Science, 21*(2), 101-112. doi:10.1007/BF02894421

Wisdom, J. P., Chor, K. H. B., Hoagwood, K. E., & Horwitz, S. M. (2014). Innovation adoption: a review of theories and constructs. *Administration and Policy in Mental Health, 41*(4), 480-502. doi:10.1007/s10488-013-0486-4

Yusuf, Y., Gunasekaran, A., & Abthorpe, M. S. (2004). Enterprise information systems project implementation: A case study of ERP in Rolls-Royce. *International Journal of Production Economics, 87*(3), 251-266. doi:10.1016/j.ijpe.2003.10.004

ACKNOWLEDGEMENTS

I wrote this book during a two-year period of extensive travel throughout the United States. Among the many aspects of the country for which I now have a greater appreciation are the local institutions that contribute to vibrant community life, even in the most remote places. In particular, I am indebted to the many public libraries that provided a quiet place to write and cherished internet access.

Additionally, I am grateful to the organizations and colleagues with whom I have worked over the last two decades; without them, I never would have learned the implementation lessons I share in this book.

Finally, unending thanks to Curtis and Rufus, my partners in travel and life, whose support helped transform a book idea into an actual book.

ABOUT THE AUTHOR

Wendy Hirsch is a consultant and coach who helps organizations and individuals master the art and science of change. Her implementation experience spans two decades and includes work in nonprofit, for-profit, and government sectors in the United States and around the globe. To learn more about Wendy and her work, visit wendyhirsch.com.

Printed in Great Britain
by Amazon